Contents

Chapter 1: Digital issues

Chapter 2: Our digital future

Introduction

The Internet of Things is Volume 299 in the **ISSUES** series. The aim of the series is to offer current, diverse information about important issues in our world, from a UK perspective.

ABOUT THE INTERNET OF THINGS

The Internet is not just the Internet anymore. Products ranging from smartwatches and TVs to cars and fridges all use the Internet to connect our daily lives. This book explores the rise of the Internet of things, from the negative consequences of online technology to positive innovations. Articles include debate over screen-time for young children, online privacy and access to broadband. They also examine our digital future, looking at advancements in robot law and social applications.

OUR SOURCES

Titles in the **ISSUES** series are designed to function as educational resource books, providing a balanced overview of a specific subject.

The information in our books is comprised of facts, articles and opinions from many different sources, including:

⇨ Newspaper reports and opinion pieces

⇨ Website factsheets

⇨ Magazine and journal articles

⇨ Statistics and surveys

⇨ Government reports

⇨ Literature from special interest groups.

A NOTE ON CRITICAL EVALUATION

Because the information reprinted here is from a number of different sources, readers should bear in mind the origin of the text and whether the source is likely to have a particular bias when presenting information (or when conducting their research). It is hoped that, as you read about the many aspects of the issues explored in this book, you will critically evaluate the information presented.

It is important that you decide whether you are being presented with facts or opinions. Does the writer give a biased or unbiased report? If an opinion is being expressed, do you agree with the writer? Is there potential bias to the 'facts' or statistics behind an article?

ASSIGNMENTS

In the back of this book, you will find a selection of assignments designed to help you engage with the articles you have been reading and to explore your own opinions. Some tasks will take longer than others and there is a mixture of design, writing and research-based activities that you can complete alone or in a group.

FURTHER RESEARCH

At the end of each article we have listed its source and a website that you can visit if you would like to conduct your own research. Please remember to critically evaluate any sources that you consult and consider whether the information you are viewing is accurate and unbiased.

Useful weblinks

www.ageuk.org.uk

www.barnardos.org.uk

www.bournemouth.ac.uk

www.cardiff.ac.uk

www.childnet.com

consumers.ofcom.org.uk

www.theconversation.com

digi.me

http://edtechnology.co.uk/

www.theguardian.com

www.huffingtonpost.co.uk

www.independent.co.uk

www.newelectronics.co.uk

www.nominettrust.org.uk

www.pcadvisor.co.uk

www.pewinternet.org

www.rsnonline.org.uk

www.swnsdigital.com

www.telegraph.co.uk

www.yougov.co.uk

The Internet of Things

Series Editor: Cara Acred

Volume 299

MidKent College
LEARNING RESOURCE CENTRE
Medway Campus

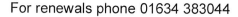

Independence Educational Publishers

First published by Independence Educational Publishers

The Studio, High Green

Great Shelford

Cambridge CB22 5EG

England

© Independence 2016

ISBN-13: 978 1 86168 740 1

Printed in Great Britain
Zenith Print Group

Youth and the Internet

By Jonathan Rallings

It is sometimes difficult for older generations to properly appreciate just how quickly the environment young people are growing up in today is being changed by technology. Even relatively young adults in their thirties came of age in an era where mobile phones were the sole preserve of bankers or wealthier estate agents, whilst the Internet was an emerging novelty, slow and periodically accessible via dial-up modems accessed largely in institutions rather than the home.

For young people in 2015, though, life without information and communications technology seems as unfathomable and quaint as an era before sliced bread. Unlike any previous generation in history, young people today have instant access to the sum of human knowledge and information through the click of a mouse. This provides unparalleled opportunities for learning, global connection and innovation as never before. But alongside the numerous benefits bestowed by the Internet, it is increasingly clear that the potential for relentless and all-consuming contact with the virtual world is also presenting new and unpredictable challenges for young people.

Something that does not appear to have changed is the basic challenge of adolescence with its attendant emotions, anxiety and obsessions. Baroness Beeban Kidron's informative documentary *InRealLife* (2013) – looking at this very issue of how the Internet is impacting on youth – shows clearly that teenagers today, speaking in their own words, are still recognisably teenagers as most of us would describe them (often from our own personal experience). What has altered drastically, though, is the level of risk that young people may potentially expose themselves to when growing up due to the extremes to which the consequences of teenage behaviour can be magnified when facilitated by the Internet. This is illustrated all too clearly in the film by poignant interviews with young people reflecting on addictions to pornography and gaming they have developed from their Internet use, or, perhaps most shockingly, the young woman exchanging sexual favours in order to retrieve a stolen phone.

Just as in the 'offline' world, we are learning that cyberspace also presents its own bespoke dangers to child well-being which as a society we are only just beginning to acknowledge and react to. And the reality is that it is the most vulnerable, less likely to have attentive parents to supervise them, and often lacking basic education, who are most exposed to the dangers that advancing technology poses – the Internet in particular. These young people, who have always been most at risk of problems such as addiction or exploitation, now face greater extremes in terms of the consequences of their actions due to the Internet. Increasingly, disturbing case studies of sexual exploitation and sexual abuse are linked to Internet 'grooming' of vulnerable young people – not only to facilitate 'contact' abuse by arranging to meet up in real life, but increasingly through the soliciting of explicit imagery via social media or the incitement of sexual activity on webcams. These are serious safeguarding concerns.

Well my lovely little marvel of technology... Just keep my reputation in good shape and my friends genuine ones... Thank you!

Young men experiencing a world where they can access freely available and worryingly graphic pornography online appear to be warping their understanding of both their own and young women's sexuality. There is some evidence this is also contributing to both genders' expectations of relationships and what is accepted as 'normal' is being altered – leading to a potentially regressive twist in the quest for gender equality. Even young people themselves are expressing their concerns about pornography in the Internet age, with an Institute for Public Policy Research (IPPR) survey finding 80% of young people saying it was too easy to access pornography online, and 72% feeling that it is leading to unrealistic views about sex – particularly among boys. Although the Government has recently moved to encourage Internet Service Providers to offer content filters which restrict access to various explicit material online, it is not clear yet how effective this strategy will be in helping keep young people safe online not only from pornography but other disturbing sites promoting self-harm or suicide for example.

The same report also found that 46% of 18-year-olds felt that sending naked pictures to each other – a practice more commonly known as 'sexting' – was "part of everyday life for teenagers nowadays". Given teenage hormones it is not exceptionally surprising that young people should be using technology in this way, but not all will be fully equipped to consider the future consequences of their actions. Barnardo's own internal research has found that some young people gather as many as 2,500 'friends' on social networking sites – as a sign of status. But this can present major risks when these 'friends' can often be less trustworthy than the young person assumes and private photos are suddenly effectively public in the hands of others. The term 'revenge porn' is now common parlance as intimate pictures of what are mostly young women are placed online as an act of humiliating vengeance, usually after a relationship breakdown. Previous generations have taken for granted the ability to emerge from adolescence with embarrassing adolescent mistakes mostly forgotten. But for today's young people, most of whom are publicly sharing their lives through social media, their teenage indiscretions are possibly likely to remain readily accessible for the rest of their lives – including by employers. It is still uncertain how far this may present itself as a disadvantage going forward.

The issue of sexting is one element of the wider phenomenon of cyber-bullying which experts are increasingly concerned is affecting the lives of many children and young people. In previous generations children who were bullied at, say, school would be likely to find refuge at home over the weekends or during school holidays. But in a world of instant connection and social media, vulnerable young people are increasingly finding themselves tormented day and night with little or no respite. It is concerning but not surprising to find that agencies such as ChildLine are suggesting that calls to them about cyberbullying (up 87%) and sexting/pornography (up 145%) are increasing at alarming rates.

It is important to remember, though, that the Internet still represents a vastly positive advance for young people – which is perhaps why it is valued so highly by them. *InRealLife*, for example, documents the positive engagement of connection between hundreds of young video bloggers – 'vloggers' – convening on Hyde Park to meet each other for the first time after connecting online. It shows a sensitive and supportive relationship between two young gay men discovering their sexuality at opposite ends of the country who may never have otherwise found each other. It might equally have contrasted the vastly improved access to knowledge and information today's schoolchildren benefit from. Or the way in which individual stories can now touch the lives of many people in ways not seen before, such as that of Stephen Sutton, the young man whose online videos of bravery and optimism in face of terminal cancer led to millions of pounds being raised for charity as well as undoubtedly raising awareness of cancer risks for countless young people.

This all emphasises how the Internet has brought amazing opportunities for young people – to learn, to interact and to allow them a greater sense of their relation to a globalised world. Social media and content platforms such as YouTube, Vine or Vimeo are allowing young people to communicate in ways like never before – to connect and create together. Young people appear to be increasingly creating and inhabiting their own world of media, distinct from the mainstream, with some attracting millions of followers, achieving the sort of fame and influence among their peers which previous generations would only have attached to film or rock stars.

The benefits for young people can be enormous – as it facilitates greater peer-to-peer learning than was ever possible before. It is a space where even the most isolated and vulnerable young people, or those coping with

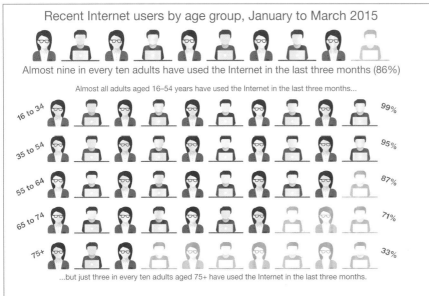

Recent Internet users by age group, January to March 2015

Almost nine in every ten adults have used the Internet in the last three months (86%)

Almost all adults aged 16–54 years have used the Internet in the last three months...

16 to 34 — 99%
35 to 54 — 95%
55 to 64 — 87%
65 to 74 — 71%
75+ — 33%

...but just three in every ten adults aged 75+ have used the Internet in the last three months.

Source: Office for National Statistics, Internet users: 2015, 22 May 2015

some of the issues discussed in this paper like identity or bullying, can find like minded friends and communities to validate and make them feel less isolated. There is also a vast quantity of information – both official and informal – to allow young people to cope with their 'growing pains' which in previous times may have isolated them.

That is not to say that this new world of connectivity does not raise big questions about peer pressure and privacy. Whereas previous generations were subject to peer pressure largely confined to small communities within towns or schools, now young people are confronted with comparing themselves to their peer group on a global scale. It is not clear what impact this may or may not be having as yet, but it is difficult to imagine that it does not from time to time cause insecurities in even the most confident teenagers. Even the biggest fish must sometimes feel small when swimming in the largest possible pond.

Contrary to popular belief, it seems young people are actually more concerned about their online privacy than other generations, being more likely to check and adjust privacy settings on the Internet than other, older, age groups. This is hardly that surprising for a generation which is increasingly aware that one misjudged photo or comment online may affect their job prospects or happiness for the rest of their lives. It also helps to explain the popularity among young people of apps specifically designed to prevent an archivable record for the future – like Snapchat, which allows a photograph to be sent which is then ostensibly deleted automatically after a momentary amount of time (usually six seconds). However, even Snapchat is not immune to breaches of privacy, after it emerged last year that third party apps had allowed messages to be intercepted and 'screen grabs' taken, resulting in user photos being saved and stored. This has served to further underline the maxim that, really, nothing that is posted on the Internet should ever be assumed to be 'deletable'.

So young people are seemingly caught between two opposing and contradictory forces – one drives them to share online as much as possible to keep up with their peers, whilst the other emphasises the potential pitfalls that one wrong move on social media etc. might lead to. It is unknown what strain this might be putting young people under and what impact it may be having on the mental health of some, even at the same time that the Internet is so celebrated and cherished by teenagers generally.

The positivity that the Internet can bring to young people's lives, though, must challenge the temptation for older generations to instinctively consider the Internet as ultimately threatening to childhood. The reality is that like any other technical advance, there are likely to be myriad positives and negatives experienced by young people at an individual level. For example, an over reliance on electronic communication by some young people may be viewed negatively by some, concerned about the importance of interpersonal skills to success in life. But we must remember there have always been young people less comfortable with oral or interpersonal communication who are now more likely to value online communication as offering the benefit of more time and space to think through and write their thoughts in a considered way without feeling a need for an immediate response. Equally it should be remembered interpersonal skills may become considerably less important in an economy immersed in social media and online communication anyway.

Following her experiences making *InRealLife* Baroness Kidron has pulled together a proposal for a series of 'iRights' – basic rights which children and young people should expect when going online (see box, bottom right).

May 2015

⇨ The above information is reprinted with kind permission from Barnardo's. Please visit www.barnardos.org.uk for further information.

iRights

The right to remove:

Every child and young person under the age of 18 should have the right to easily edit or delete any and all content they themselves have created.

The right to know:

Children and young people have the right to know who is holding and profiting from their information, what their information is being used for and whether it is being copied, sold or traded.

The right to safety and support:

Children and young people should be confident that they will be protected from illegal practices, and supported if confronted by troubling or upsetting scenarios online.

The right to make informed and conscious choices (agency):

Children and young people should be free to reach into creative and participatory places online, using digital technologies as tools, but at the same time have the capacity to disengage at will.

The right to digital literacy:

To access the knowledge that the Internet can deliver, children and young people need to be taught the skills to use and critique digital technologies effectively, and given the tools to negotiate emerging social norms.

Smartphones, tablets and Facebook are the best inventions of the 21st century

For everyone, the smartphone is the stand-out invention of the century so far – but young people stress the importance of Wikipedia and YouTube.

By Will Dahlgreen

In only 15 years, technology has changed beyond recognition. In 2000 the most popular phone was the Nokia 3310; in 2004 a computer processor might have 170 million transistors, while in 2013 it had 4.3 billion; and with the rise of digital the US music market is worth almost three times less than in 2004. Some downplay the rate of change ushered in by the Internet – one argument is the telegraph reduced message transmission from three weeks to 30 minutes, while the Internet has reduced it from 30 seconds (with fax) to two. But it's the breadth of change that's truly revolutionary: by 2020 around 70% of the world's population are forecast to have a smartphone in their pocket.

There's no doubt among British people that the smartphone is this century's best consumer invention so far – over twice as many choose it as any other. Although preceded by the Blackberry, the iPhone was the first smartphone to popularise a touchscreen, and with the first truly popular tablet computer also designed by Apple – chosen as the second most significant invention – Apple is perhaps this century's greatest pioneer.

In August 2015 a billion people used Facebook on a single day, a seventh of the world's population. Facebook is seen as the third most significant consumer invention, chosen by 23%.

Facebook doesn't have the same cross-generation appeal as the smartphone or tablet, however. While every age-group place the smartphone first and all but the youngest place the tablet in their top three, Facebook is only the fifth most important invention for 40–59s and over-60s, but comes second for the younger generations.

Likewise, Wikipedia has disproportionately revolutionised the lives of young people. In 2014 we found that fully 84% of 18–24s had used Wikipedia for professional or academic research, compared to only 49% of 40–59 year olds. It's seen as the joint-third most important invention to the youngest generation, tied with YouTube (23% each), which only 3% of over-60s see as an important invention.

In contrast, the top two generations say video messaging service Skype, which has helped millions connect with their children while at university, overseas or having moved away from home for work, is the third most important invention. They also stress the importance of TomTom and other automotive navigation systems, both placing this in fourth.

26 January 2016

⇨ The above information is reprinted with kind permission from YouGov. Please visit www.yougov.co.uk for further information.

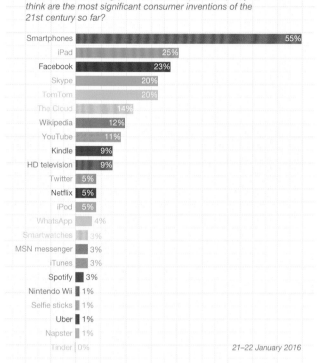

The best inventions of the 21st century
Which of the following (or other-brand equivalents) do you think are the most significant consumer inventions of the 21st century so far?

Smartphones	55%
iPad	25%
Facebook	23%
Skype	20%
TomTom	20%
The Cloud	14%
Wikipedia	12%
YouTube	11%
Kindle	9%
HD television	9%
Twitter	5%
Netflix	5%
iPod	5%
WhatsApp	4%
Smartwatches	3%
MSN messenger	3%
iTunes	3%
Spotify	3%
Nintendo Wii	1%
Selfie sticks	1%
Uber	1%
Napster	1%
Tinder	0%

21–22 January 2016

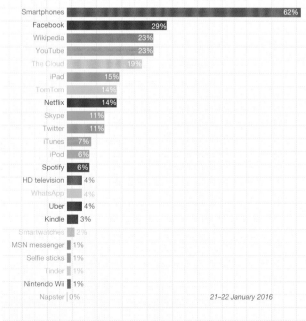

Generational views of the 21st century
% of 18- to 24-year-olds who choose the following (or other brand equivalents) as the most significant consumer inventions of the 21st century

Smartphones	62%
Facebook	29%
Wikipedia	23%
YouTube	23%
The Cloud	19%
iPad	15%
TomTom	14%
Netflix	14%
Skype	11%
Twitter	11%
iTunes	7%
iPod	6%
Spotify	6%
HD television	4%
WhatsApp	4%
Uber	4%
Kindle	3%
Smartwatches	2%
MSN messenger	1%
Selfie sticks	1%
Tinder	1%
Nintendo Wii	1%
Napster	0%

21–22 January 2016

Young people's experiences with in-app purchases

An online survey of over 1,000 young people aged 11 to 18 explores young people's experiences with in-app purchases, finding that over one in ten respondents had accidentally spent money on an in-app purchase.

Smartphones are the most popular device among 11-18s

Smartphones emerged as the most popular device when respondents aged 11–18 years were asked which devices they use on a weekly basis. 82% of 11–18-year-old respondents said that they used a smartphone on a weekly basis, compared to 9% who said they use a normal mobile on a weekly basis. Other popular devices include tablets (61%), laptops (58%), gaming devices (46%), computers (43%) and smart TVs (37%). Just 1.3% said they don't use any of these devices on a weekly basis.

Young people's use of apps

Downloading apps emerged as a common experience among 11–18-year-old respondents, with 95% saying they had downloaded an app. Spending money on apps is less common, but nonetheless, over half of respondents (59%) said they had paid for an app and over a third (37%) said they had spent money on an in-app purchase. Interestingly, boys responding to the survey were significantly more likely than girls to report that they had paid for an app (67% vs 50%) and paid for an in-app purchase (45% vs 28%), while there were few other reported gender differences.

Accidental spending on in-app purchases

A significant minority of the young people responding to this survey said they have accidentally spent money on in-app purchases. 12% said they have accidentally spent money on an in-app purchase, while 7% said they have received a big phone bill has a result of accidental in-app purchases.

Respondents who had accidentally spent money on their phone or tablet were invited to share more background about what happened.

The most common response was that they thought that it was free; for example, they didn't realise the costs associated with it or didn't realise it was real money.

Another key reason given as the cause of accidental in-app purchases, was that they accidentally clicked on the purchase.

Many young people shared how they were caught out because details, including passwords, had been automatically stored and there wasn't a prompt for the user to give confirmation.

There were also a number of cases where young people pressed the button too many times as it didn't seem to be working. Interestingly, it was observed that all of these situations were reported by boys.

Other specific cases highlight the range of ways that young people can accidentally spend money on an in-app purchase.

Other spending via mobiles

33% said they have voted for a contestant on TV and 18% said they have entered a competition by call or text.

26% said they have made a text donation to charity.

Girls are significantly more likely than boys to have voted for a TV contestant (42% vs 26%), entered a competition by call or text (22% vs 16%) or made a text donation to charity (30% vs 22%).

Parents are paying for the bills...

83% said their parent pays their phone bill, while 17% said they pay for their bill themselves. There are no statistically significant gender differences.

... and parents are the most important source of support

Parents are by far the most important source of support if young people are worried about unknown costs on their phone bill. 89% said they would turn to a parent/carer, while other sources of support include other family members (13%), friends (11%) and siblings (10%). Just 3% said they would turn to a teacher, while 7% said there is no one they would turn to. There are no statistically significant gender differences.

⇨ The above information is reprinted with kind permission from Childnet. Please visit www.childnet.com for further information.

Techie teens shaping communications

A 'millennium generation' of 14- and 15-year-olds are the most technology-savvy in the UK, according to new Ofcom research, which shows that after our teens our digital confidence begins a long decline.

Teens born at the turn of the millennium are unlikely to have known 'dial-up' Internet and are the first generation to benefit from broadband and digital communications while growing up.

The research – part of Ofcom's 11th *Communications Market Report* – measures confidence and knowledge of communications technology to calculate an individual's 'Digital Quotient' score, or 'DQ', with the average UK adult scoring 100.

The study, among nearly 2,000 adults and 800 children, finds that six year olds claim to have the same understanding of communications technology as 45-year-olds. Also, more than 60% of people aged 55 and over have a below average 'DQ' score.

It shows that we hit our peak confidence and understanding of digital communications and technology when we are in our mid-teens; this drops gradually up to our late 50s and then falls rapidly from 60 and beyond.

The study helps support Ofcom's duty to research the markets it

regulates and better understand people's technology literacy.

As a result of growing up in the digital age, 12- to 15-year-olds are developing fundamentally different communication habits than older generations, even compared to the advanced 16-24 age group.

Children aged 12–15 are turning away from talking on the telephone. Just 3% of their communications time is spent making voice calls, while the vast majority (94%) is text based – such as instant messaging and social networking.

By contrast, older generations still find it good to talk: 20% of UK adults' communications time is spent on the phone on average. While adults also embrace digital text-based communications, the traditional email is most popular (used for 33% of their time spent communicating) compared to just 2% among 12–15s.

We're communicating more than sleeping

It's not only younger teens that are making the most of digital communications technology. Ofcom's research shows that the communications habits of adults of all ages are shifting as they embrace newer services and take advantage of portable connected devices.

The average UK adult now spends more time using media or communications (8 hours 41 minutes) than they do sleeping (8 hours 21 minutes – the UK average).

But because we're squeezing more into our day by multi-tasking on different devices, total use of media and

communications averaged over 11 hours every day in 2014. This is an increase of more than two hours since Ofcom last conducted similar research in 2010.

Since then, we're even better connected through superfast broadband and 4G mobile, and communicating on the move.

Among the adult population, it's the 16–24s who spend the most time on media and communications. They're cramming over 14 hours of media and communications activity into 9 hours 8 minutes each day by multi-tasking, using different media and devices at the same time.

Tied to our tablets and smartphones

Where computer use was traditionally dependent on desktop computers, tablet and smartphone devices are starting to dominate how we work and play. Over four in ten households (44%) now have a tablet – up from a quarter (24%) a year ago.

Their ease of use and portability appeal to people across generations. More than a quarter (28%) of those over 55 now own a tablet and many use it as their main computing device.

Young adults are glued to their smartphones for 3 hours 36 minutes each day, nearly three times the 1 hour 22 minute average across all adults.

Smartphone take-up has also continued to increase rapidly over the past year, up to six in ten adults (61%), compared to half (51%) a year earlier. The growth in smartphone use in particular has contributed to people spending an extra two hours per day on media and communications since 2010.

We're holding on to our books, CDs and DVDs

Despite the growth in digital media and devices, people are holding on

to popular forms of physical media such as books, CDs and DVDs.

The average-sized DVD and Blu-ray disc collection increased from 45 to 68 discs per person between 2005 and 2014.

Books remain the most popular physical media – 84% of UK adults had a physical book collection in April 2014, down from 93% in 2005. Books are more popular than DVD/Blu-ray discs (80% own a collection, from 81% in 2005) and music CDs (79% this year, down from 92% in 2005).

The average size of a book collection fell by three books to 86 per person, while the average size of a music CD collection declined by six CDs to 84.

Ownership of music CDs varies greatly between age groups. Some 60% of people aged 16–24 were significantly less likely to own music CDs than all other age groups. However, among 45- to 54-year-olds, almost nine in ten (88%) were likely to own a music CD collection.

The number of books owned increases with age. The largest printed book collections were held by those aged 55 to 64 years old, with an average of 118 books. The smallest average collection size was that of 16- to 24-year-olds with an average of 50 books each.

Technology and work-life balance

While technology is seen by many as a distraction in our daily lives, a quarter (24%) of workers think technology is improving their work-life balance. Just under half (49%) say it is not making much difference either way and 16% think technology is making their work-life balance worse.

Six in ten (60%) workers do some form of work-related communications activity outside of working hours. Emailing is the most common work-based communication activity out of hours, with nearly half (46%) of all workers emailing from time to time, and a fifth (22%) doing so on a regular basis.

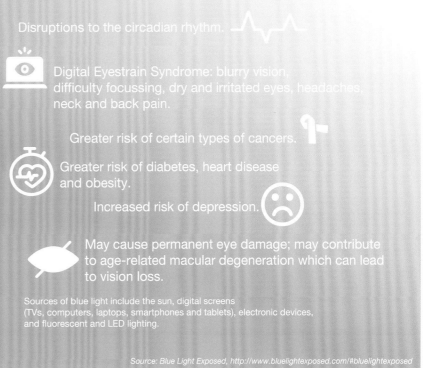

Harmful effects of blue light

Disruptions to the circadian rhythm.

Digital Eyestrain Syndrome: blurry vision, difficulty focussing, dry and irritated eyes, headaches, neck and back pain.

Greater risk of certain types of cancers.

Greater risk of diabetes, heart disease and obesity.

Increased risk of depression.

May cause permanent eye damage; may contribute to age-related macular degeneration which can lead to vision loss.

Sources of blue light include the sun, digital screens (TVs, computers, laptops, smartphones and tablets), electronic devices, and fluorescent and LED lighting.

Source: Blue Light Exposed, http://www.bluelightexposed.com/#bluelightexposed

Around four in ten workers are also taking part in work-related telephone calls (41%) and text messages (37%) occasionally outside their working hours.

The largest proportion of work-related communications takes place in the evening at home. Of those people, one in ten read or send work emails or texts in bed, on waking in the morning or last thing at night.

Communications technology is also shaping our holiday time. The research shows almost a third (32%) of people have made work related calls, sent emails or texts while on holiday, and of those, one in ten has worked on the beach, or by the pool.

But there is a trade-off. Six in ten workers say that while they're at work they regularly or occasionally send and receive texts for personal reasons; half of workers use email; while 46% make or receive telephone calls for non-work related reasons. Just over a quarter (27%) catch up on the sports results at work, while one in five people are shopping online in the office.

Ed Richards, Ofcom Chief Executive, said: "Our research shows that a

'millennium generation' is shaping communications habits for the future. While children and teenagers are the most digitally-savvy, all age groups are benefitting from new technology.

"We're now spending more time using media or communications than sleeping. The convenience and simplicity of smartphones and tablets are helping us cram more activities into our daily lives."

James Thickett, Ofcom Director of Research, said: "While gadgets can prove a distraction, technology is actually improving work-life balance for some.

"Six in ten of us do some form of working outside of normal hours, but the trade-off is that we're making personal calls and doing our life-admin at work."

6 August 2014

⇨ The above information is reprinted with kind permission from Ofcom. Please visit consumers.ofcom.org.uk for further information.

One in four teenagers are being trolled and abused online

One in four teenagers were subjected to abuse online in the last year, a major report has revealed.

By Lucy Sherriff

A survey of 13- to 18-year-olds found 24% reported they were targeted on the Internet because of their gender, sexual orientation, race, religion, disability or transgender identity.

One in 25 said they are singled out for abuse "all or most of the time".

The alarming findings emerged in a study published to mark Safer Internet Day.

It revealed that more than four in five (82%) youngsters have seen or heard "online hate" in the previous 12 months, with 41% suggesting it had become more rife.

Researchers defined online hate as behaviour targeting people or communities via the Internet because of their gender, transgender identity, sexual orientation, disability, race, ethnicity, nationality or religion.

It could be offensive, mean or threatening, and either targeted directly at a person or group, or generally shared online. In its most extreme form it can break the law and become a hate crime.

Social media platforms were the most common domains in which youngsters witnessed hate on the Internet, according to the report.

It said youngsters with disabilities and those from black, Asian, Middle Eastern or other minority ethnic communities were more likely to see online hate.

The survey of more than 1,500 teenagers also found 93% of respondents have seen their friends posting supportive, kind or positive content about a certain group in the last year.

Will Gardner, chief executive of the charity Childnet and director of the UK Safer Internet Centre, which published the study, said: "While it is encouraging to see that almost all young people believe no one should be targeted with online hate, and heartening to hear about the ways young people are using technology to take positive action online to empower each other and spread kindness, we were surprised and concerned to see that so many had been exposed to online hate in the last year.

"It is a wake-up call for all of us to play our part in helping create a better Internet for all, to ensure that everyone can benefit from the opportunities that technology provides for building mutual respect and dialogue, facilitating rights, and empowering everyone to be able to express themselves and be themselves online – whoever they are."

Peter Wanless, chief executive of the NSPCC, said the Internet industry has a duty to keep young people safe.

"Socialising online is central to children and young people's lives today, so it's very worrying that so many are witnessing or experiencing online hate," he said.

Education Secretary Nicky Morgan said: "The Internet is a powerful tool which can have brilliant and virtually limitless benefits, but it must be used sensibly and safely.

"We are working hard to make the web a safer place for children but we can't do it alone and parents have a vital role to play in educating young people."

Online abuse and cyberbullying have emerged as major issues alongside the explosion in popularity of social media sites.

Last year figures showed convictions for crimes under a law to prosecute Internet 'trolls' have increased eight-fold in a decade.

9 February 2016

⇨ The above information is reprinted with kind permission from The Huffington Post UK. Please visit www. huffingtonpost.co.uk for further information.

Britain opts out of EU law setting social media age of consent at 16

Facebook, Snapchat and Instagram will be able to process data of anyone 13 and over after agreement reached.

By James Titcomb

The UK will opt out of European privacy laws that require under-16s to get parents' permission to use Facebook and other social media after a compromise deal on sweeping data protection legislation.

The proposed rules will set the age of consent for Internet services that use personal data, including email, social media and apps at 16, instead of 13 as in many countries around the world. As originally planned, it would have meant millions of teenagers requiring permission to use popular Internet services including Facebook, Snapchat and Instagram.

But a compromise reached on Tuesday night will allow individual countries to apply their own laws on the age of consent. The Government said it would maintain current laws allowing those aged 13 and older to use Internet services, in line with many other countries around the world.

An amendment inserted into long-awaited data protection rules last week said that "the processing of personal data of a child below the age of 16" would require parental consent, but the final text says that a member state can have this age as low as 13.

"Concerns have been listened to and the UK's age of consent will not be forced to change," said Conservative

MEP Timothy Kirkhope, who led negotiations for the European Conservatives and Reformists group.

Raising the age of consent to 16 would have caused a major headache for Internet services and apps like Facebook, Instagram, Snapchat, Google and Twitter, which currently have minimum ages of 13. The technology industry had warned against the proposals, as had Internet bullying groups who warned that it could lead to children lying about their age.

Facebook's minimum age has been 13 since 2006, when it was reduced from 17.

Failure to abide by the laws can mean tough penalties of up to 4 per cent of global turnover. These could mean tens of millions of pounds for the biggest Internet companies. The law is due to be voted on in the new year and come into force two years late.

16 December 2015

⇨ The above information is reprinted with kind permission from *The Telegraph*. Please visit www.telegraph.co.uk for further information.

Digital dangers

Summary of Digital Dangers: the impact of technology on the sexual abuse and exploitation of children and young people.

Barnardo's and Marie Collins Foundation. Authored by Tink Palmer, 2015

Research conducted with a number of Barnardo's services, both specialist child sexual exploitation and educational services, has revealed how integral new technology has become in the sexual abuse and exploitation of children. The Internet and new technologies have allowed potential victims to be accessible and available to perpetrators, who may be anonymous, quickly and freely in ways that would otherwise not be possible. Children and young people are now able to communicate more easily with people they would otherwise not usually interact with.

Children and young people at risk of harm online may not have any previous vulnerabilities that are often associated with being victims of sexual abuse and exploitation, such as being in care, from families facing adversities or having a history of sexual abuse. This means that they are less likely to be identified as they might not be known to the authorities. Also, because of the nature of online activity the currently accepted indicators of possible sexual exploitation, such as going missing or school absence, may not be displayed, and the first parents may know that their child has been a victim of sexual exploitation is when the police contact the family.

Certain groups of children and young people, such as young people with learning difficulties, those with mental health problems, lesbian, gay bi-sexual, transgender and inquisitive young people, appear to be particularly vulnerable to online harm.

All professionals interviewed for the research believed that the development of new technology over the last 11 years has changed the way they have to work with young people and the methods of providing support.

The report highlights the need for:

⇨ Easier access to existing prevention resources and advice, including age-appropriate healthy relationships and sex education through schools

⇨ Training for all professionals working with children and young people so that they feel confident in identifying those at risk of harm online

⇨ Assessments to be carried out by support services to include abuse that relates to online harm only

⇨ Assessment of products, such as games and apps, both those currently in use and those in development, to make sure they have safeguards in place to prevent children being harmed online.

2015

⇨ The above information is reprinted with kind permission from Barnardo's. Please visit www.barnardos.org.uk for further information.

Through which ONE of the following ways do you think you would find it **easier** to express your feelings or views?

Country	Using words	Using emojis	Using a combination of words and emojis
Czech	58%	13%	22%
Germany	47%	11%	35%
Greece	48%	10%	36%
Ireland	48%	6%	43%
Italy	33%	13%	50%
The Netherlands	47%	18%	31%
New Zealand	54%	8%	35%
South Africa	60%	10%	25%
Spain	36%	10%	48%
UK	48%	9%	33%
USA	47%	7%	40%

% of people who agree with the following statement: *"Cyberbullying is worse than bullying face to face/ in person."*

Country	%
Czech	51%
Germany	51%
Greece	46%
Ireland	60%
Italy	48%
Netherlands	51%
New Zealand	55%
South Africa	64%
Spain	53%
UK	35%
USA	42%

Source: Groundbreaking Vodaphone global survey reveals 43% of teens think cyberbullying a bigger problem than drug abuse, Vodaphone, 22 September 2015

Separating a student from their iPhone can be bad for their health and for their brain

THE CONVERSATION

*An article from **The Conversation**.*

By Gary W. Lewandowski Jr Chair/Professor of Psychology, Monmouth University

If you forgot your phone at home, you may get a sense of being incomplete in some way, the itch you just can't scratch each time you reach for your absentee phone. Our phones have become such an integral part of our lives that they feel like they are part of us. Your phone is where your mind goes during a less than captivating business meeting, a boring class or a family function. Surely you are missing something – a text, an Instagram update, a tweet from Kanye. The possibilities are endless.

Can being away from your phone really have a negative effect on you? To answer that question, researchers advertised a study which allegedly focused on completing word searches and blood pressure. The advert attracted 40 college students who arrived individually and were fitted with a blood-pressure cuff, then worked for five minutes finding the 50 US states within a large word-search puzzle. The more states they found, the more money they would have a chance to win.

Participants were randomly assigned to either complete the puzzle either with or without their iPhone. Those in the 'no iPhone' group were informed by the researcher that the phone caused interference with the blood pressure equipment. The researcher, making sure the phone's ringer remained 'on', then placed the phone in an adjoining cubicle about four feet away, where the participants could still easily see and hear their phone.

Three minutes into the word-search exercise the researcher called the participant's phone and allowed it to ring six times before hanging up – which took approximately 20 seconds. At the four-minute mark, researchers took blood-pressure measurements and then stopped the participant at five minutes.

Those allowed to keep their phones were asked to switch them to 'silent mode' while working on the word search. They had their blood pressure measured at four minutes, and were stopped at five minutes.

The participants completed two different word searches, once with their phone and once without, after which they were asked to choose statements that matched their levels of anxiety (for example: "I feel tense") and the extent to which the iPhone was part of their sense of self (for example: "My iPhone is central to my identity").

As predicted, participants felt their iPhone was a greater part of their identity when it was in their possession as opposed to when they were separated from it. When participants were away from their phones the results indicate that they felt greater anxiety, had higher blood pressure, increased heart rate and performed less proficiently on the word search task (in terms of the number of states they could find).

The researchers also looked to see whether amount of daily iPhone use by participants influenced the results, but found there was no difference between those who said they use their phone a lot in their everyday lives and those who only use their phone a little.

Fear of missing out

The results suggest that being separated from your ringing iPhone has negative consequences for your cognitive performance, your feelings of anxiety – and can even effect you physiologically.

The findings on the detrimental effects on cognitive performance are consistent with other research on how mobile phones and texting affect a driver's ability to pay attention. These results are also consistent with other findings that the mere presence of a mobile phone can undermine face-to-face conversation and result in less trust.

There are caveats: the first is that the researchers only used 40 participants when a larger sample would have made the results more convincing. The use of college students may be particularly problematic for the interpretation of these results, as college students may be more attached to their phone than the average person. Finally, the study only focused on iPhones and iPhone users, but it is likely that these results would apply to users of other smartphones as well.

This study provides some compelling initial evidence that our relationship with our phones is likely to be different from the relationships we have with other electronics – such as our TV or laptop. Given the fact that an increasing number of people are using them more and more, it would pay for us to understand these phenomena better.

16 January 2015

⇨ The above information is reprinted with kind permission from *The Conversation*. Please visit www.theconversation.com for further information.

Want to get a good night's sleep, kids?

The impact of social media on young people's lives is underlined today as a new study by researchers from the University-based Wales Institute of Social and Economic Research Data (WISERD) reports that more than one in five teenagers say they "almost always" wake up during the night to look at or post messages.

In a paper being presented to the British Educational Research Association (BERA) by researchers at WISERD, the report also reveals that more than a third of 12- to 15-year-olds say they do so at least once a week.

Unsurprisingly, this is revealed to be having knock-on effects on how tired the youngsters feel at school: among some children it may even be more important than having a late bedtime in creating feelings of fatigue.

The sleep-disrupting use of social media at night also seems to be impacting on pupils' overall happiness, with lower levels of well-being reported by those who wake to use social networks.

Meanwhile, the study also has implications for the debate on whether teenagers should be allowed to start school later, to give them more time to sleep in the morning. The research team say their data suggest such a change could do more harm than good.

The team's findings on teenage sleep patterns are drawn from statistical analysis of a survey of 412 pupils in year eight (aged 12 and 13) and 436 pupils in year ten (aged 14 and 15), educated in secondary schools across Wales.

The adolescents were asked how often they wake at night to use social media. Some 22 per cent of year eight pupils, and 23 per cent among those in year ten, answered "almost always".

A further 14 per cent of the younger group, and 15 per cent of the older, said they did so at least once a week.

Those surveyed were also asked how often they felt tired at school.

More than half of those who reported "almost always" waking to use social media also said they "almost always" go to school feeling tired.

This was much higher than the overall percentage of respondents saying they "almost always" feel tired at school, which was 32 per cent among year eight pupils and 39 per cent among year tens.

The study found substantial proportions of pupils reporting going to bed very late: 17 per cent of year eight and 28 per cent of year tens said they put their heads down at midnight or later on a school night. Among these, six per cent of the younger group and eight per cent of the older claimed to go to bed later than one am.

However, the study found that, in the case of the younger group, the amount of time spent in bed actually seemed less important, in terms of whether the child then reported feeling tired at school, than whether they woke up during the night to use social media.

This was not the case among the older group. However, even among this group, those saying they woke up to use social media every night were still twice as likely to say they were constantly tired than those who never did so.

The researchers also found a strong association between pupils reporting having a regular time when they woke up in the morning and not feeling tired.

WISERD's Dr Kimberly Horton, who is presenting research on Wednesday, said: "Having a regular waketime and using social media during the night appear to be more important in determining whether a young person is always tired during the day than the time they go to bed, how long they spend in bed and having a regular bedtime.

"It seems [very] important to discourage adolescents from using social media during the night. No amount of effort to develop regular bedtimes or to lengthen the time in bed would seem to be able to compensate for the disruption that this can cause."

Last week, Paul Kelley, a former headteacher now working at Oxford University's Sleep and Circadian Neuroscience Institute, told the British Science Festival that school start times should be put back to combat sleep-deprivation among pupils.

But the WISERD paper argues against later school start times. It says that pupils would be less likely to have regular waking times as a result, reiterating that routine waking times seemed from the survey data to be very important in terms of making a child less likely to feel tired.

The paper says: "Having a regular morning routine may actually prove to be a very important feature in helping adolescents concentrate and enjoy their learning, something that may actually be undermined by changes to the school day."

Sleep patterns also seem to have a clear impact on pupils' overall reported level of wellbeing. The pupils were asked how happy they were, on a scale of one to seven. Among the younger pupils, those who reported nearly always feeling tired were nearly a point less happy on average, while among the older group, those reporting as nearly always tired were half a point less happy.

Routines and rest: the sleep behaviours of 12 to 15 year olds, a paper by Dr Kimberley Horton, Professor Chris Taylor and Professor Sally Power, all of the Wales Institute of Social and Economic Research, Data and Methods and Cardiff University, was presented to BERA on Wednesday, 16 September.

15 September 2015

⇨ The above information is reprinted with kind permission from Cardiff University. Please visit www.cardiff.ac.uk for further information.

© Cardiff University 2016

Getting your fix: technology addiction

In today's world, technology is a vital fix for many kinds of problem. But, increasingly, it is becoming another kind of fix – and problem – for probably millions of people worldwide. Technology brings with it a powerful addiction.

By David Boothroyd

'Internet addiction disorder' (IAD) is coming to be recognised widely by the medical profession and governments as a serious problem to the extent that one version, relating to gaming, is listed in the latest version of the psychiatrists' Bible, the *Diagnostic and Statistical Manual of Mental Disorders*, or DSM. Meanwhile, the US Academy of Paediatrics has published guidelines regarding children and use of the Internet.

Gaming is seen as the prime culprit, but Internet – or, more generally, technology – addiction can involve several other kinds of content supplied by today's digital technologies on various devices; for example, social media and pornography. Many academics are now studying the problem, one of them being Phil Reed, Professor of Psychology in Swansea University's College of Human and Health Sciences.

"The signs are very similar to other activities, such as gambling. People spend increasing amounts of time on the net, social media and so on – more time than they want to – and find themselves brushing off friends and family. This starts to impact their lives in a negative way." Another sign is disrupted sleep: studies have shown people are waking up to check Facebook in the middle of the night.

"There is some evidence to suggest the addiction has a negative impact on health," Prof. Reed says. "We don't understand this properly yet, but it's something to do with a lack of face-to-face interaction, which is known to boost your immune system. If you are spending increased amounts of time online on a solitary pursuit, then you don't see that immunity boost effect.

"Technology addiction can be associated with increases in depression and social isolation and, in part, that is because a lot of people who are technology addicted have an unmet need. That might be for social contact and they think the net is going to give it to them; but it doesn't. So they get more and more depressed and socially isolated, and it becomes a vicious circle."

The person credited with being the first to see the emergence of technology addiction is psychologist Dr Kimberly Young, who began to study the topic as long ago as 1995 and wrote in 1998 a book called *Caught in the Net*. She has founded netaddiction.com and the Center for Internet Addiction Recovery. She compares online addiction to drugs or alcohol, because the Internet provides addicts with the same kind of 'high' and they become dependent on it to feel normal.

How big a problem is it?

"In Europe and North America, prevalence looks like somewhere around four or 5% of the younger population (16 to 30)," Prof. Reed says. "In Asia, you might triple that figure. We don't know why that is the case.

"Internet addicts often know there is a problem but, as with most addictions, it is very difficult to own up to; there is still a bit of shame about it. We have demonstrated ourselves withdrawal effects (a study last year by Swansea and Milan University was the first to show this). When addicts come offline, they get negative mood swings, increased levels of depression and increased impulsivity.

"We have also found a wide range of physiological effects. When I first started talking about this, I used to say it was a bit like being addicted to ecstasy. I now think that was wrong; it's more like heroin in the sense that the physiological effects you get from withdrawal are somewhat similar to other sedatives.

"With sedatives, once you stop taking them, opposite kinds of effects occur; your blood pressure goes up and you become tense. And that is what we are seeing with the net."

Some countries, notably South Korea, are considering passing legislation to try to control harmful use of technology, for example by limiting advertising. A separate bill proposes to take 1% of the gaming industry's revenue to create a fund to curb addiction. While the bill has found favour with the likes of parents, religious leaders and the medical profession, it has alarmed the Internet industry and enraged gamers. A law passed in 2011 already bans gaming between midnight and dawn for anyone under age 16, but is being appealed at South Korea's Constitutional Court.

One notorious case that took place in Korea in 2010 was the death of a baby girl from malnutrition, said to be the result of obsessive use of the Internet by the parents. The man was sentenced to two years in jail. This, and other events, prompted the government to study the subject of Internet game addiction and its latest survey reported that 2% of Koreans aged ten to 19 – around 125,000 people – needed treatment for excessive gaming or addiction. This in a country where games are broadcast live on TV to audiences of millions.

Other countries, like China, Australia, Singapore and Japan, have also sounded similar warnings that Internet addiction represents a significant health threat.

Evidence is also growing that technology addiction is affecting the brain. For example, a paper published in the scientific journal *PLOS One* showed the condition is associated with structural abnormalities in the brain. "Grey matter volumes … and white matter changes … were significantly correlated with the duration of Internet addiction in the adolescents with IAD," said the authors.

Another academic paper, published in *Current Psychiatry Review* in 2012, says IAD "ruins lives by causing neurological complications, psychological disturbances and social problems". The paper goes on to claim there is increasing evidence that there can be a genetic predisposition to addictive behaviours and that the symptoms show overlap with other behavioural addictions.

Another doctor trying to help technology addicts is Dr Henrietta Bowden-Jones, honorary senior lecturer in the Division of Brain Science at London University's Imperial College and founder and director of the National Problem Gambling Clinic based in London. This is the UK's only NHS clinic for problem gambling.

Gaming is definitely the most common technology addiction problem area, she says.

"Such people are typically obsessed with the activity. They think about it virtually all the time; even when not playing. They suffer from irritability, anxiety or depression if they are stopped from playing and spend more and more time playing, isolated from other people."

One reason gaming is thought to be the worst culprit for addiction stems from the nature of the activity itself; an inherently competitive process structured to create winners, which is known to stimulate neurobiological reward mechanisms (the release of dopamine) in the brain.

Apart from gaming, the other major problem area for technology addiction is gambling, although this was obviously an activity that has caused addiction problems for many years before the Internet appeared.

At the moment, there is no treatment for Internet addiction available on the NHS, although there are private clinics that provide such services.

"I think there is a need for that and the NHS should provide it at some point," says Dr Bowden-Jones. "We are developing some treatment protocols and would love to use them but, currently, there is no funding available to treat Internet gaming addicts. It would be great to see a centre of excellence established. If someone goes to their doctor today for treatment, they will probably be referred to see a psychological counsellor, who will typically offer a form of cognitive behavioural therapy."

Looking at the problem from the slightly broader view of 'technology dependence' is Remy Oudghiri, French director of the Trends and Insights Department at market research company Ipsos (Ipsos MORI in the UK). His team has researched how many people consider themselves to be dependent on it.

"The number of such people has increased over the last five years. In most advanced countries, around 80% of people need to connect every day, otherwise they cannot work, communicate or do lots of their everyday tasks."

Oudghiri feels a turning point occurred around 2010, when the smartphone revolution took off.

"A major consequence was that people became connected all the time and, in our survey, some 10% go to sleep with their mobiles, saying they 'feel more secure'."

He says the situation poses a key question for us all: how can we keep control in a society that is becoming hyper connected, where being connected is not just a possibility, but an obligation and a necessity? How to do this is the subject of a book by Oudghiri published last year.

"Our surveys show an increasing proportion of people say they are losing control due to a lack of time, concentration or creativity. There is always a 'lack' and, when you try to dig deeper, there is a direct correlation to their use of technology."

Clearly, technology addiction is a growing problem, even if the vast majority of us manage to use technology without getting addicted. But it might just be that the powerful

attraction of electronic games could be put to positive use. This is certainly the view of the man whom many see as the father of gaming. Atari founder Nolan Bushnell has formed a new company, called Brainrush, to exploit the power of games as an educational tool.

Bushnell believes that combining gaming techniques with brain science will change education more in the next five years than it has in the last 3,000. "It's a perfect storm," he says.

Jesse Schell, CEO of Schell Games, who has taught at Carnegie Mellon's Entertainment Technology Center, says it is already happening, with educational games being the fastest growing part of the market.

"People see the power that games hold. They see the engagement. Parents say 'I wish they were as excited about algebra as they are about *Call of Duty*'."

Similarly, a project targeted at girls and underway at Northeastern University in Seattle has a self-explanatory acronym: GAMES – Girls Advancing in Maths, Engineering and Science. There is already something of a track record for this approach, with some hugely successful girl-oriented games. For example, Seattle-based Her Interactive has sold more than nine million copies of one such game.

Finally, the Center for Game Science at the University of Washington specialises in developing scientific discovery games and cognitive skill training games.

From whatever viewpoint, addiction or education, electronic game playing is clearly no longer a trivial matter.

23 April 2014

⇨ The above information is reprinted with kind permission from David Boothroyd, NewElectronics. Please visit www.newelectronics.co.uk for further information.

The Internet hasn't killed privacy – but it has changed it forever

THE CONVERSATION

An article from **The Conversation.**

By Jose Such, Lecturer in Cyber Security, Lancaster University

Disclosure statement: Jose Such receives funding from EPSRC as part of the RePriCo project.

When people say "privacy is dead", it's usually for one of two reasons. Either they truly believe that privacy is irrelevant or unachievable in today's hyper-connected world or, more often, that not enough is being done to protect privacy when huge amounts of personal information are being posted online. Although I agree more could be done to protect privacy online, I believe that privacy is not dead, it's just changing forms.

While it's true that we're sharing more information online than ever before, this doesn't mean that we no longer care about privacy. On the contrary, some curious trends in how users share information on social media suggest we're actually becoming more cautious.

Back in the early 2000s when the first social networks MySpace and Facebook appeared online, users were much more open with their personal information. Most had 'public' profiles, which could be accessed by anyone, and few cared much about privacy.

But a host of high-profile incidents have flashed through the mainstream media in the last decade. People have been fired from their jobs, had their secrets revealed, divorced and cyberbullied because of content on Facebook. So it's no wonder that users began to understand the perils of poor management of their online privacy, and that Facebook users in particular have become more protective of their personal information. Recent research proved that people are increasingly limiting the data that is publicly shared with other Facebook users.

Generation gap

Despite these trends, parents of today's teens are particularly worried about how their children manage their presence online. The 2013 PEW report on teens, social media and privacy, found that only 9% of teens were concerned about third-party access to their data on Facebook, while 80% of parents expressed high levels of concern about it.

Young people are certainly sharing more information about themselves through social media than before, and they sometimes get caught out. Recently, a 14-year-old boy who sent a naked photo of himself to a girl on Snapchat found that the incident had been recorded by police.

But perhaps parents could have a little more faith – the same report indicates that teens are being vigilant about their online privacy in different ways. The researchers found that: 74% of teens had unfriended and 58% had blocked other users to avoid sharing information with them; 60% of teens kept their profile private; 58% said they shared inside jokes or cloaked their messages in some way; 57% decided not to post something online because it may have had negative consequences for them in the future; and 26% reported false information to help protect their privacy.

Multi-party menace

But there are some privacy issues that can't be addressed by adjusting user settings or sharing in-jokes. Privacy is no longer only about what you say or disclose about yourself online. It's also about what others say or disclose about you. Privacy is becoming a collective phenomenon.

At the moment, mainstream social media only gives control over privacy settings to those who upload photos – not those who are in them. Take a simple but illustrative example: if Alice uploads a photo of her and Bob, Alice is the one who controls who gets to see the photo. But if Bob doesn't want Alice's friends to see him, it's up to him to get Alice to take the photo down, or else report it to the site administrator.

At the University of Lancaster, we have been looking at how multi-party privacy conflicts emerge, and how we might be able to solve them. We're conducting large-scale studies of a 1,000 social media users to help us develop the next generation of privacy tools and empower users who find themselves in these scenarios.

Privacy will keep changing forms in the future – particularly as new technologies are created, existing ones mature and users' perceptions of privacy evolve. The biggest challenge will be to make sure that users have the tools they need to keep up with these changes, and protect their privacy as they see fit.

17 September 2015

⇨ The above information is reprinted with kind permission from *The Conversation*. Please visit www.theconversation.com for further information.

Parents, is it OK to spy on your child's online search history?

Microsoft's Windows 10 and other parental control software face criticism for harming teens' exploration of sensitive topics such as sexuality.

Can giving parents detailed activity reports of their child's online search terms be harmful to young people looking for information on sensitive topics such as religion, sexuality, gender or domestic abuse?

When Microsoft this summer launched its new Windows 10 feature that lets parents see what their children get up to online, this was one of the criticisms it encountered.

Microsoft has since welcomed feedback and promised an update, with more appropriate default settings for teenagers. However, it is not the only service provider offering this level of parental control. Most security software companies today sell 'family' products, many including reports, notifications and video supervision. But is it right to spy on your child?

The UN Convention on the Rights of the Child stipulates that children have a right to privacy and a right to information. They also have a right to protection from all types of violence and exploitation – and there lies the rub.

With a young generation more Internet-savvy than their parents, ensuring online safety for minors

surfing an ever-expanding web becomes a hard task. Today's parents don't have an older generation to turn to for tech advice, so many turn to parental control software instead.

Recent research commissioned for Norton by Symantec, a provider of antivirus and security software, shows that 46% of British parents worry that they don't know what their children are doing online.

Nick Shaw, Norton's general manager of Europe, the Middle East and Africa, is one of those worrying parents. Perhaps predictably, he uses parental control software, including reports.

"I'm not looking at what they're doing day to day, I'm just checking to make sure that they're safe," he says. He emphasises that he uses Norton's family feature alongside face-to-face discussions with his children, and encourages other parents to do the same.

Raj Samani, chief technology officer at Intel Security, previously McAfee, applies a family protection pack with informed consent and says his children approve of his monitoring because he is transparent about the reasons for it.

"My daughter tried to communicate with somebody and I got the notification. And actually what she was doing was unsafe so I ended up having a conversation with her, explaining the concept of anonymity."

Shaw and Samani both have children aged 11–16, the age that 61% of British parents believe is when their children are most vulnerable online. Shaw says parents' product demands depend on their child's age: parents of young children often want to monitor screen time, whereas those with teenagers raise concerns about social media.

"We build a tool that allows parents flexibility to do what they want," says Shaw.

Samani says parents and children do need to have a discussion about when monitoring should stop: "To me I think it comes down to a point where you have got that level of understanding and maturity."

Cyber security consultant Dr Jessica Barker questions whether parental monitoring is fair on children, and says it can intrude into their privacy. Referencing research by Professor Sonia Livingstone on Internet governance and children's rights, she goes so far as to say it can be harmful.

"If [children] feel they are being monitored that undermines any kind of relationship of trust. They might be using the Internet in a healthy way to get information and support, and feel that they are not able to do that because they are being monitored."

She brings up the issue of teenagers wanting to explore their gender or sexuality in private. If parents have a problem with that, or even use filters blocking LGBT sites, that could cut off access to something hugely helpful, a service previous generations didn't have.

One young man, who wants to remain anonymous, said that his homosexuality was outed to his unsupportive parents by parental control software.

"They didn't say they had seen what I had looked at but they hinted very strongly at it in conversation," he said, adding that he soon learned how to work around his parent's system.

Barker says: "There's certainly evidence that suggests that teenagers who know they are being monitored at home will look at a friend's device. And then they don't have someone to talk to about it."

So do software companies consider these issues when creating their services?

"Absolutely," says Samani. "We'll always recommend that the reporting and the communication for children should be used as a vehicle to begin or continue that dialogue with children.

Shaw says Norton "looks at every aspect when designing a tool", but adds that the primary focus is protecting the child. "At the end of the day it's a tool … How people use the tool is up to them."

When it comes to balancing privacy and protection, the key concepts that emerge are education, conversation, consent and the fact that the Internet offers lots of opportunities for children – positive and negative. As for how far parental control should go, our anonymous gay man sums it up well: "Computers shouldn't do the parenting."

5 November 2015

⇨ The above information is reprinted with kind permission from *The Guardian*. Please visit www.theguardian.com for further information.

Bringing their own future

Helen Dorritt explores how primary and secondary schools are harnessing BYOD for the benefit of learning.

When mobile phones first became a ubiquitous part of day-to-day life, they were an immediate distraction for students, and teachers battled to keep them out of the classroom. But with the advent of smartphones and tablets creating instant access to limitless information and resources, more and more schools are changing their attitudes to these beeping interlopers and actually embracing their presence through BYOD – bring your own device.

YouGov research from 2014 shows that 81% of UK 13–18-year-olds own their own smartphone, with 34% also owning a tablet. Primary-aged children are equally tech savvy, with statistics from the same year recording that 25% of children own their own tablet before the age of eight and 70% are confident in using mobile devices by the time they go to school. So whether you like it or not, there's no getting away from the fact that technology is an intrinsic part of life today, and more and more schools are realising the benefits of integrating it into their teaching in order to benefit learning. "The way that students work on a day-to-day basis is completely different now," says Brian Fischer, assistant headteacher of Tibshelf Community School. "They expect access to Wi-Fi at all times and to be able to use their devices."

BYOD is a simple idea: students bring in their own smartphones, tablets and laptops for use in the classroom. Teachers can plan a lesson around them, or use them in a more spontaneous manner to encourage independent research. Tablets for Schools, a charity that helps schools use the transformative powers of technology to build learning and attainment, has done a great deal of research into the benefits of using devices in the classroom and records that: "Many learning benefits were apparent soon after tablets were introduced,

from greater engagement through to independent learning, communication, collaboration and content that could be customised for different learning styles and abilities. Students themselves reported learning benefits."

Tibshelf, a secondary school in Derbyshire, is currently exploring the benefits of BYOD for its 700 students. The school moved into new premises in 2013 and took this opportunity to integrate technology into its everyday teaching practice, of which BYOD was a part from the beginning. "We started out small, asking students to use their devices to undertake research in lessons," explains Brian. "For example, if a student wants to know something, we encourage them to take out their phone and find it out for themselves. This also has the advantage of lessons being more spontaneous and allowing teachers to react to events in class – they don't have to have planned everything in advance. It's also useful for students to be able to access simple apps such as dictionaries and calculators."

In terms of more complex functions, Tibshelf is trialling a free student planner app, where homework assignments can be automatically uploaded to a student's network profile by teachers, and that parents can also access to check what work their child should be doing. There have also been some unexpected uses of BYOD that teachers hadn't predicted. "We've found that some students are taking photos of things on the board, such as diagrams or equations, as it's a quick and easy way to capture information." Tibshelf's BYOD scheme has been received enthusiastically by its students, with 95% of them accessing the network – some even accessed it on Christmas Day! "They love it, and see having Wi-Fi at school as a massive bonus."

In addition to educational benefits, there's no denying the financial benefit too: with budgets shrinking more every year, schools are often unable to provide students with up-to-date devices for use in the classroom, so having them use their own is a simple and cost-effective way to obtain and maintain equipment that's fit for purpose. Recent research by the British Educational Suppliers' Association shows that 81% of schools would 'consider' using BYOD and 16% would 'prefer' it to bulk-buying equipment for the school. "We've also found that no student has ever broken their own device," says Brian. "And generally what they own is better than what we could provide."

When using BYOD in a school setting, then the infrastructure is vital. Tibshelf worked closely with its chosen ICT providers, the Stone Group, to build a system that would be able to support a multitude of devices being used all at once, that would work for both Apple and Android platforms and that would stop devices from bringing viruses into the school system. "Security was also a huge concern for us," says Brian. "We needed it to be completely secure, with no chance of it being hacked." The students' server is therefore separate from the staff one, so sensitive information is not accessible.

As well as keeping the network safe, the ability to keep devices secure is also vital, so the issue of storage needs to be considered. LapSafe Products manufactures trolleys and lockers for just this very purpose, and which have the added bonus of being able to charge devices too. "It's important to ensure that you provide the right kind of storage, security and availability of lockers as well as a number of charging methods to support the multitude of devices available today," says Mark Exley, LapSafe's Business Development Director.

"Not all devices are the same, and that must be considered when introducing BYOD into a school; you must provide a universal solution that is manageable, scalable and, of course, cost effective." The company will work closely with a school and its staff to establish a BYOD storage and charging solution that works for them. There are clearly a myriad of positive benefits of such a system, but what problems has Tibshelf encountered? "Student misuse and how to deal with it is the biggest issue," explains Brian. "So we made it clear from the beginning that the teacher has to ask students to bring out their devices – it's not a given assumption in every lesson. As a carrot, we gave permission for students to use the Wi-Fi at break times for personal use, but the stick is that if they misuse the system in class, we can instantly cut off their access."

Getting all of the staff on board had to be considered as well, as some were more reticent to implement it into their teaching practice than others due to concerns about abuse of the system and its appropriateness in a school setting. "We didn't enforce it," Brian says. "Teachers had the option to use it or not. But my attitude is, if something is better than what you already have, why wouldn't you use it?"

Another concern of BYOD is that not all students come from the same economic background, meaning that they may not own their own device, or could have a cheaper version. This could lead to both bullying from other students and also be an educational disadvantage. To overcome this, Tablets for Schools recommends that schools operate a financial support strategy which offers loans, lease-to-own schemes, grants or donations.

Brian has some tips to share with other schools who might be thinking of bringing in BYOD. "A good network is vital; one that is secure and has the capability to handle a large number of devices on it. I would suggest getting in experts who know the field well rather than doing things in-house – I can't recommend the Stone Group enough. You have to sell the idea of BYOD to staff, so involve them from the very beginning and allay any fears they may have. Share some ideas with them on how to use it in their lessons. Once you've got some wins and positive uses, you'll be able to build on these. We're really pleased with how it's going and what it can be used for in the future."

17 June 2015

⇨ The above information is reprinted with kind permission from Education Technology. Please visit http://edtechnology. co.uk for further information.

How much screen time is healthy for children? Expert tips on screen safety, education, mental development and sleep

New research reveals four in five parents believe gadgets aid their child's development, but how much screen time is healthy? Guidelines to reduce a child's screen time for health, psychological and educational benefits.

By Simon Jary

Many parents are under the belief that technology and gadgets are essential for a child's development, but can you go too far? How much time should a child spend in front of a screen is a question being asked not just by worried parents but psychologists, health organisations and even governments. Read an expert's guidelines for managing a child's screen time, and his warnings on the dangers of recreational screen time, especially before bedtime.

A new TLF Panel survey conducted on behalf of kids clothing retailer Vertbaudet.co.uk found that four in five parents believe technology and gadgets are good for kids, aiding in their development. The study found that 37 per cent of parents asked said that their child spent between one and two hours a day playing with tech gadgets, and 28 per cent said between two and three hours. Moreover, the study found that 38 per cent of two- to five-year-olds own an Android tablet, and 32 per cent own an iPad; almost a third (32 per cent) of these kids also have a mobile phone.

The reason behind all this gadget use: over a third of parents (35 per cent) said they use tech gadgets to entertain their children because they are convenient, and nearly a quarter (23 per cent) because they want their children to be tech-savvy. A 2015 survey of 1,000 British mothers of children aged two to 12 found that 85 per cent of mums admit to using technology to keep the kids occupied while they get on with other activities.

The AO.com survey pointed to children spending on average around 17 hours a week in front of a screen – almost double the 8.8 weekly hours spent playing outside.

Wanting our children to be tech-savvy is understandable, and the need to keep them entertained will also make sense to many a parent. But we must also weigh up the risks associated with children having too much screen time.

In his lecture 'Managing Screen Time and Screen Dependency', Dr Aric Sigman argues that "whether it's Facebook, the Internet or computer games, screen time is no longer merely a cultural issue about how children spend their leisure time, nor is it confined to concern over the educational value or inappropriate content – it's a medical issue".

Sigman is concerned less with a child's ICT or Computer Science study or use of computers for homework, but more with their screen time in non-educational environments in front of entertainment screen media such as television, the Internet and computer games. He has some strong recommendations for reducing children's screen time, from toddlers to teenagers – and adults, too.

Obviously he is less worried by educational television programmes and even some educational computer games or mobile apps, but still recommends strictly limiting all screen time for kids.

TV has been an easy 'babysitter' for years now, aided even further with DVDs, Netflix and so on. But computer, tablet and mobile screens

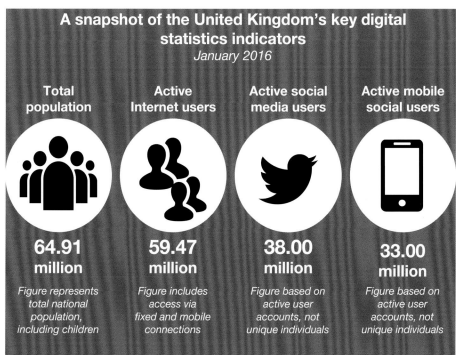

A snapshot of the United Kingdom's key digital statistics indicators
January 2016

Total population	Active Internet users	Active social media users	Active mobile social users
64.91 million	**59.47 million**	**38.00 million**	**33.00 million**
Figure represents total national population, including children	*Figure includes access via fixed and mobile connections*	*Figure based on active user accounts, not unique individuals*	*Figure based on active user accounts, not unique individuals*

Information compiled by We Are Social, visit http://wearesocial.com/uk/special-reports/digital-in-2016
Sources: UN; US Census Bureau; ITU; Facebook; G SMA Intlligence.

engender more worry, in what has been put down as merely the latest generational complaint – "fresh expressions of horrible and timeless anxieties ... a tried and true form of advanced-age self-care".

The current generation of children in most Western societies spends more time in front of a screen than any before it. A study back in 2010 – before even the phenomenal rise of Apple's iPad and other tablets – estimated that by the age of ten, children had access to an average of five screens in their lives. That number, Sigman suggests, has almost certainly risen since.

In addition to the main family TV, for example, many young children have their own bedroom telly along with portable computer game consoles (Nintendo, PlayStation, Xbox), smartphone, family computer and a laptop and/or a tablet computer.

By the age of seven the average child will have spent a full year of 24-hour days watching recreational screen media, claims Sigman. Over the course of childhood, children spend more time watching TV than they spend in school.

More screens means more consumption, and more medical problems argues Dr Sigman.

Effect on academic grades

In 2015, Cambridge University researchers recorded the activities of more than 800 14-year-olds and analysed their GCSE results at 16. Those spending an extra hour a day on screens (TV, computer, games console, phone) saw a fall in GCSE results equivalent to two grades overall.

On average, the 14-year-olds said they spent four hours of their leisure time each day watching TV or in front of a computer.

An additional hour of screen-time each day was associated with 9.3 fewer GCSE points at 16 – the equivalent of dropping a grade in two subjects. Two extra hours of screen-time was associated with 18 fewer points – or dropping a grade in four subjects. Even if pupils spent more time studying, more time spent watching TV or online still harmed their results, the analysis suggested.

Establish screen time rules

So how much screen time is healthy for a seven-year-old, ten-year-old, even one-, two- or three-year-old? How much TV should a child watch? How many hours in front of a computer? You may be shocked too at how much time in front of a screen has an adverse effect on a child's health and development.

Parents who want to reduce their children's screen time need to establish rules to reduce the risk of later health and psychological issues.

Sigman admits that there is a lack of clarity of advice, but points to a number of governmental advice points on the maximum amount of time a child should spend in front of a screen.

In 2013, the US Department of Health recommended that children under two years of age should not be in front of a screen at all, and over that age the maximum leisure screen time should be no more than two hours a day.

The French Government has even banned digital terrestrial TV aimed at all children under three, while Australia and Canada have similar recommendations and guidelines.

Taiwanese parents are now legally obligated to monitor their children's screen time. The Taiwanese government can levy £1,000 fines on parents of children under the age of 18 who are using electronic devices for extended periods of times. Similar measures exist in China and South Korea that aim to limit screen time to a healthy level.

The UK Government has recently backtracked on a 2008 guidance that children should be exposed to technology and computers from a very young age, but there is currently no medical or governmental guidelines on screen time in the UK.

In a 2012 report on media consumption in the UK Ofcom estimated that the average three- to four-year-old spends three hours a day in front of a screen. This rises to four hours for ages five to seven, 4.5 hours by ages eight to 11, and 6.5 hours for teenagers.

The report also found that older children are spending more time online and are more likely to go online alone, children aged 12–15 are spending more time online (rising from 14.9 hours a week to 17.1 hours) and spend as much time in a week using the Internet as they do watching television. Up to 43 per cent of kids are

also more likely to mostly use the Internet in their bedrooms.

Children who use the Internet mostly alone comprise one in seven Internet users aged five to seven (14%), one in four aged eight to 11 (24%) and over half of those aged 12–15 (55%).

Children are going online via a wider range of devices. Internet access using a PC or laptop is increasingly being supplemented by access through other devices. All age groups are more likely in 2012 to go online using a tablet computer, and children aged five to seven and 12-15 are also more likely to go online using a mobile phone.

Addiction dangers of too much screen time early in life

"Early screen viewing is likely to lead to long periods of viewing for the rest of your life," says Sigman. "The way you view screens when you are young forms the habits you pick up forever after it seems."

An early taste for entertainment screen media can lead to changes in the brain that stay with you for life – a life that may be shorter as a result.

Like other addictions screen time creates significant changes in brain chemistry – most notably, in the release of dopamine. This neurotransmitter – also known as the pleasure chemical – is central to addictions from sugar to cocaine.

"Dopamine is produced when we see something that is interesting or new, but it also has a second function. Dopamine is also the neurochemical involved in most addictions – it's the reward chemical.

"There are concerns among neuroscientists that this dopamine being produced every single day for many years – through for example playing computer games – may change the reward circuitry in a child's brain and make them more dependent on screen media," warns Sigman.

What happens in an Internet minute?

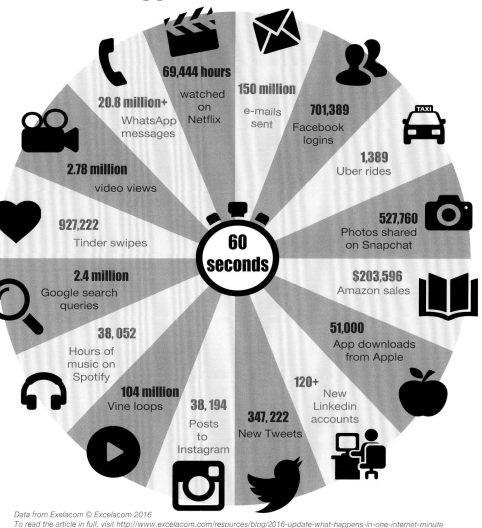

Data from Exelacom © Excelacom 2016
To read the article in full, visit http://www.excelacom.com/resources/blog/2016-update-what-happens-in-one-internet-minute

On the perils of too much screen time, Sigman has investigated the extent to which time online may be displacing face-to-face contact, and that lack of social connection is associated with physiological changes, increased incidence of illness and higher premature mortality?

Dangers of childhood computer gaming

Think about the type of games children are getting addicted to playing. The narrative of a game is an important factor, as some – *Grand Theft Auto* being the obvious example – clearly lead to a lack of impulse control, and potential neurochemical changes in the release of dopamine.

"Providing a child with a lot of novelty may produce higher levels of dopamine in a child's brain, making the child seek more and more screen time to satisfy their need for more dopamine," says Sigman.

An article in the *American Journal of Drug and Alcohol Abuse* suggested that "computer game playing may lead to long-term changes in the reward circuitry that resemble the effects of substance dependence".

"Computer game addicts or gamblers show reduced dopamine response to stimuli associated with their addiction presumably due to sensitisation."

Games in a virtual world also lead to a false sense of competence. Children need to base their lives on reality not fake, virtual worlds, says Sigman.

Sigman is also sceptical about the supposed benefits of computer game play, such as better hand-eye co-ordination. There may well be improved eye-hand-keyboard-mouse dexterity but many reports of such benefits are sponsored by interested games and tech companies, he claims.

Fast use of a games console controller is of little use outside of the gaming environment. And the reduction in sustained attention is a far greater loss.

Catherine Steiner-Adair, a clinical psychologist and author of *The Big Disconnect: Protecting Childhood and Family Relationships in the Digital Age*, disagrees that increased screen time is good for children and young adults. Children who are heavy users of electronics may become adept at multitasking, she argues, but they lose the ability to focus on what is most important – a trait critical to the deep thought and problem solving needed in life.

Screen time effects on educational development

Children's cognitive development is two years down on what it was 30 years ago because children have lost both concrete and abstract thinking.

Today's children have less idea of weight and length measurements because the more time spent in virtual worlds, the less they are involved in the real world. This is the finding from two expert reports from 2007 and 2009: *Thirty years on – a large anti-Flynn effect? The Piagetian test* **Volume & Heaviness** *norms* by Michael Shayer and Denise Ginsburg.

Sigman is critical of schools over-use of technology, which he blames on the multi-billion-pound education-tech industry forcing its products on schools and even nurseries on the unfounded fear that children suffer without using the latest digital devices.

"Until we know better, I advise precaution," says Sigman. "Keep technology and screens away from the under-threes, and set limits on all ages after that."

With so many dangers associated with too much screen time for children, and little fixed advice from health authorities or governments Dr Sigman offers his own guidelines (see below) for reducing the risks.

Tablets before bedtime cause sleep disruption

Sigman was recently interviewed on British TV – watch the clip here – about how the use of tablets and other electronic devices can disrupt children's sleep – indeed adults' sleep will also be affected by what is known as 'Blue Light' that these tech products emit.

The light from digital devices is 'short-wavelength-enriched,' so it has a higher concentration of blue light than natural light – and blue light affects levels of the sleep-inducing hormone melatonin more than any other wavelength.

"Recreational screen time has now moved into the bedroom," warned Sigman.

"There is a strong link between tablet or any type of small screen that emits what is known as 'blue light' – good in the morning as it wakes us up; bad in the night as it wakes us up.

"The Kindle Paperwhite doesn't emit the same levels of blue light. And there are filter glasses and apps that actually change the type of light, but light isn't the only reason.

"Brains are being stimulated before bedtime in the way that books don't do. Exciting games just before bedtime is not a good idea. Electronic devices should be switched off at least an hour before bedtime," the expert warns.

It's not necessarily all bad

Experts who regard some screen time as beneficial urge parents to pay attention to how their kids act during and after watching TV, playing video games, or on the computer online. "If they're using high-quality, age-appropriate media, their behaviour

is positive, and their screen-time activities are balanced with plenty of healthy screen-free ones, there's no need to worry."

But even these parents should consider creating a schedule that works for their family: including weekly screen-time limits, limits on the kinds of screens they can use, and guidelines on the types of activities they can do or programmes they can watch. See our guidelines below.

It's important to get your kids' input as well – media literacy and self-regulation help buy in. It's also a great opportunity to discover what your kids like watching, letting you introduce new shows and apps for them to try.

So how much screen time for children?

The simple answer: not much. None for children under two. That's right. The experts suggest that babies and toddlers are kept away from all screens. Sorry *CBeebies*.

Children aged two to five years should have no more than an hour a day, and children aged five to 18 years should have no more than two hours a day. That's a tough call for teenagers, especially with homework often requiring computer time. But remember that the real danger is non-educational, leisure screen time, so you may wish to discount homework screen time.

Parents should be able to decide if these strictures are too harsh, and allow some screen time flexibility, but not caring at all about the amount of time your children spend in front of screens is dangerous.

17 November 2015

⇨ The above information is reprinted with kind permission from PC Advisor. Please visit www.pcadvisor.co.uk for further information.

How the Internet changed my life

Jan Tchamani is one of the 2013 joint Age UK Internet Champions – here she explains how the Internet has changed her life.

I always love it when Age UK asks me to put on my Internet Champion hat and write something about this subject, so dear to my heart!

I became an Age UK Internet Champion back in March, and since then – more than ever – I've been championing the cause of getting the over-50s out there and into the digital wonderland where I spend so much of my time.

When I'm not surfing the net for useful stuff about gardening (my newest passion), or gifts for family and friends, I'm here at my desk writing blogs (a kind of online diary) or posting photos on Facebook. And I'm campaigning for the IT needs of the over-50s to be addressed in Birmingham.

My world would be so much smaller and less efficient without this amazing machine I'm typing on right now. Last weekend, my husband Terry and I celebrated our first wedding anniversary, and the whole delightful break was booked online: hotel, outings and candle-light dinners.

I can't begin to tell you how useful it was to know that, in spite of arthritic knees and a dodgy back, I would be able to comfortably manage everything.

How it all started

Ten years ago I was an English teacher in an inner city comprehensive school in Birmingham. I loved my job, but I suddenly found myself diagnosed with what they used to call 'manic depression' – bipolar – and I was no longer able to work.

Fortunately, I had been forced to get to grips with the Internet. All teachers attend regular training sessions. And sometimes you get a little extra push. Bipolar people are creative thinkers, and I remember the day when the head teacher took me on one side and said, "Jan – I love all your ideas, but you're going to have to email them to me from now on!". So I had no choice, and I find that's often the way of things.

Moving on

So at the age of 50 I found myself out of work, poorly, and 'stuck' at home with only the computer for company. It was then that the Internet became my best friend.

Lucky me: even on days when I couldn't go out or talk to anyone, I had a way of escape. I could listen to music, watch films, play adventure games and explore the world safely. What a blessing that was! And I could also learn about handling my complex health issues.

I joined Bipolar UK's 'online forum', and typed my questions into a little box on my screen. Back came a deluge of encouraging answers from fellow sufferers.

In a forum, you don't use your real name and you can really be honest. Gradually, I got back my taste for life.

Freedom for me – but what about the others?

When you go through tough times, you meet others who are facing similar challenges. Thinking about other people's situations inspired me to want to help.

Once I was settled on a sheltered housing scheme, I applied for Lottery funding for an IT Club, and professional tutors to help my neighbours become confident 'users'. Last year we ran an Age UK 'Spring Online' event, and this year we're going to be part of ITea and Biscuits Week.

I'm very excited: you never know who's going to walk in. Last month, 59-year-old Trevor learnt to apply for work online and now he's found the perfect job! His daughter's off to university soon, but can feel confident her dad won't be bored or lonely.

Championing 'digital inclusion'

What Age UK are doing to get us over-50s online is vitally important: trust me. Just as not having a phone 20 years ago put people at a disadvantage, not being online is having the same effect today. And society needs older people involved! We have so much wisdom to pass on to the young!

If you've never dipped a toe in the water, or you know someone who hasn't, please encourage them to come along to an ITea and Biscuits event. Half an hour will be enough to convince someone of the benefits.

You and I know that the spirit of adventure is still very strong in later life! Just because we have creaky knees doesn't mean we don't want to go on learning and exploring! So go on, give it a try. If you find you don't like it, feel free to write to me via Age UK, and I'll eat my hat – that's a promise!

⇨ The above information is reprinted with kind permission from Age UK. Please visit www.ageuk.org.uk for further information.

Three million more UK homes and businesses can now get superfast broadband

New figures show that the rollout of the government-funded superfast broadband has now reached more than three million homes and businesses.

More than three million homes and businesses have been reached by the Government's nationwide rollout of superfast broadband, figures published today (Wednesday 12 August) reveal.

The rollout is delivering superfast access – Internet speeds greater than 24 Mbps – to those properties not covered by existing commercial networks and is on track to take superfast access to 95 per cent of the UK by 2017. More than four out of five UK homes and businesses already have access to superfast speeds, and the rollout is currently reaching an additional 40,000 homes and businesses every week.

This comes following recent news that BT will make up to £129 million available to extend the Government-led rollout of superfast broadband across the UK.

Culture Secretary John Whittingdale said:

"Reaching three million properties is a huge achievement. Our rollout of superfast broadband is transforming lives up and down the country as every day thousands more homes and businesses are gaining access to superfast speeds.

"It's fantastic to see that the rollout of superfast broadband is now delivering for customers and for the taxpayer. The levels of people taking up superfast broadband in areas where we invested public money are beyond our expectations, and BT is now reimbursing the public purse to deliver further coverage across the UK. This now means that BT will be providing up to £129 million cashback for some of the most hard to reach areas."

The additional funding will be made available to local authorities to reinvest the money in providing further superfast broadband coverage to even more homes and businesses, and much earlier than originally planned. The money is being made available as a result of a clause in the contracts BT agreed with government and local authorities that allows the funding BT has received to be returned or reinvested into further coverage if take-up is better than the 20 per cent expected in BT's original business case. The higher take up rate to date has resulted in BT making a new business case assumption of reaching 30 per cent take-up in these areas."

The table above sets out the number of homes and businesses reached by the rollout of fibre-optic cable in each geographical area of the UK.

Gavin Patterson, CEO BT Group, said:

"The UK is making great progress with fibre broadband. 23 million premises are covered by BT's open access network, with three million of those enabled under the BDUK programme. Our Openreach engineers have worked tirelessly to connect some of the most remote parts of the UK, from Shetland and Hebrides to the moors of southwest England.

"The public have responded by taking up fibre in large numbers, and that's good news for those areas that haven't been reached yet. It means additional funds are being released which will enable us to go even further at no extra cost to the taxpayer and earlier than expected."

Country/ Region	Home and businesses reached by fibre (BDUK projects) as at 31 July 2015
North East	124,299
Yorkshire and the Humber	295,235
North West	384,667
East Midlands	338,709
West Midlands	220,624
South East	531,093
South West	311,758
East of England	391,095
Scotland	394,177
Wales	482,000
Northern Ireland	41,652

Environment Secretary Elizabeth Truss said:

"Our continuing investment in speedier broadband will unleash the full potential of our countryside – creating jobs, boosting exports and improving the quality of life for people living in rural communities.

By ensuring everyone has access to the same technology and services we can boost the productivity of rural areas, making it as easy to open and expand a business in some of the most beautiful parts of our countryside as it is in our cities."

12 August 2015

⇨ The above information is reprinted with kind permission from the Department for Culture, Media & Sport and The Rt Hon. John Whittingdale MP.

Rural areas "need better broadband"

A new report into broadband access shows the "dire" level of availability in rural areas, says Lib Dem leader Tim Farron.

The Westmorland and Lonsdale MP said urgent action should be taken to improve poor availability of broadband in the countryside.

It follows the release of the first report from the British Infrastructure Group of MPs, which examines broadband coverage.

Called *Broadbad*, the document shows that Mr Farron's Lake District constituency has among the slowest broadband speeds in the country.

With an average download speed of just 14.7 Mbps, it is 628th out of 650 constituencies when ranked in terms of average speeds.

Over 55% of broadband connections in the constituency are under 10 Mbps.

Ofcom, the regulatory body responsible for the telecoms sector, believe that a download speed of 10 Mbit/s is the minimum necessary for an "acceptable user experience".

According to the report, "48% of rural connections do not meet this minimum speed, leaving ordinary people and businesses lagging behind the rest of the country."

The report concludes that "poor Internet connections are costing the UK economy up to £11 billion per year".

Mr Farron said: "This report confirms what local people already know – broadband access in our area is simply not good enough.

"It is critical both for residents and businesses that access to decent broadband is extended to rural areas.

"Unfortunately, the scale of the problem is not matched by the scale of the Government's ambition.

"In urban areas the government is busy improving superfast and ultrafast broadband access, yet in rural areas there has only been a commitment to providing speeds of 10 Mbps by 2020.

"While that would be a welcome improvement on our current service, the reality is that in the modern day that is simply not enough.

"The Government must support the rural economy by providing decent broadband access to all."

The Government recently announced a new scheme offering subsidised satellite broadband to rural customers on slow connections.

The scheme was launched during December by the Department for Culture, Media & Sport.

Prime Minister David Cameron has also pledged that everyone will have a legal right to request a 10 Mbps broadband speed by 2020.

Mr Cameron said the government was putting access to fast broadband on a similar footing as other basic services.

> ## "The Government must support the rural economy by providing decent broadband access to all"

The Government would help ensure every home and business had access to fast broadband by the end of this Parliament, he said.

4 February 2016

⇨ The above information is reprinted with kind permission from the Rural Services Network. Please visit www.rsnonline.org.uk for further information.

Ringing the cinema, taping TV shows and travel agents – all falling victim to technology

Experts have unveiled a list of tasks, jobs and pastimes which have fallen victim to technology – including visiting the travel agents, checking a map and writing to pen friends. Researchers who carried out the study found that there are dozens of activities Brits no longer carry out due to the explosion of time-saving functions on smart devices.

The poll of 2,000 adults also found ringing the cinema to find out movie times, using public telephones and printing photographs are rare occurrences these days.

Gadgets such as smartphones and computers have also made using telephone directories, encyclopaedias, address books and dictionaries redundant.

The research, commissioned by business communications provider Daisy Group to mark its technology summit #DaisyWired2014, also found we no longer put classified adverts in shop windows or send love letters.

Kate O'Brien from the Daisy Group, said:

"Technology dominates modern life and so it comes as no surprise to learn there are a number of acts we no longer do as a result.

"Developments in computing, smartphones, televisions and other gadgets have made communicating with people easier and faster than ever before and it is now quicker to fire up the laptop to buy something rather than visit the shops, or talk to someone online rather than pick up the landline.

"Life is simply getting easier and faster, as experts are working all the time to find ways of conducting business more efficiently and saving time wherever possible. And this is just the beginning, with a huge range of jobs and activities being overtaken by technology.

"We're seeing librarians being replaced by 'bookbots' in academic libraries, automated trains taking the place of train drivers, Cloud software replacing accountants and robot vacuum cleaners replacing traditional cleaners for example."

The study also showed household chores such as hand washing clothes and hanging wet laundry outside in winter rarely happen now tumble dryers and washing machines have taken over.

Similarly, use of the telephone has changed dramatically – as gone are the days of saving up change for the pay phone, remembering phone numbers, reversing the charges and dialling 1471.

The bank, building society and post office now get fewer footfalls than ever before, as people are paying for car tax, paying bills and checking accounts online.

Keeping a personal diary, hand-writing essays and sending postcards also appear in the list of things Brits no longer do.

Other everyday activities and errands which have fallen by the wayside include booking tickets over the telephone, trying on shoes on the high street and buying flowers fresh from the florist.

Warming hot milk on the stove, using a pager and keeping copies of printed bank statements are also acts of the past.

Eight in ten people admit the majority of their daily activities now rely on technology in some way, believing advancements save them up to four hours a week.

Researchers found the average household now has at least five computing devices in the house, compared to just two or three five years ago.

The study also highlights the huge popularity of pocket-sized digital devices, with 18% of us using smartphones and 12% tablets for over 16–20 hours per week.

As surfing remotely online becomes an ingrained way of life, 36% also admit that they spend over 16 hours a week carrying out everyday activities such as online banking, uploading photos onto social media sites and listening to music.

Tom Cheesewright, author and futurologist who will be speaking at the #DaisyWired2014 event in May, said:

"Technology plays a part in every waking moment of our lives, as individuals, for businesses and in our homes, towns and cities.

"Smartphones do everything from waking us to monitoring our health; our offices are programmed with energy-saving software, and businesses can operate anywhere with Cloud technology.

"As those devices have become the norm in our lives, many tasks and activities have just been relegated to the past, with a surprising lack of sentimentality – simply because we demand that our gadgets keep pace with our hurried lives.

"Today our phone takes the place of our GPS, games console, remote control, iPod and TV as well as performing more traditional functions such as the egg timer, torch and spirit level.

"It's remarkable how quickly we continue to adapt to this new environment and, while we can't predict our future, we are undoubtedly helping to create it."

Top 20 activities of the past and new alternatives

1. Call cinema to check times; check cinema site or use app
2. VHS video recorder; Sky plus/box sets
3. Research holiday in travel agents; search online for holiday deals
4. Ring directory enquiries; Google phone numbers
5. Public payphones; mobile phones
6. Ring the speaking clock; check time on phone screen
7. Pay for tickets for events over the telephone; buy tickets online
8. Print photos from negatives; Instagram/Facebook and digital cameras
9. Take pics on disposable cameras; take pics with phone/iPad
10. Listen to Sony Walkman; music on phone or iPod
11. Carry spare change; use debit cards
12. Pay bills at the post office; pay bills online
13. Reverse charges in phone box; use mobile phones
14. Put a classified advert in the shop window; eBay/Craigslist
15. Buy TV listing magazines; use online alternative
16. Big fold-out maps; Satnav or Google Maps
17. Queue to get car tax in the Post Office; buy car tax online
18. Read a hard copy of the Yellow Pages; use online directories
19. Fax things; send an email attachment
20. Trawl through encyclopaedias; use Wikipedia and/or search engines.

31 March 2014

⇨ The above information is reprinted with kind permission from SWNS Digital. Please visit www.swnsdigital.com for further information.

⇨ Research conducted by Daisy Group.

The Internet of Me is here

Every day, we create vast amounts of data about ourselves. And the quantity is only going to grow and grow. The Internet Of Things will plug us in to a vast and ever-growing network of connected devices from wearable technology to domestic appliances to entire 'smart cities'.

The potential for innovation is as enormous as it is exciting. And our personal data is the fuel driving it all.

The shiny new hardware – from smartphones to sensors – is merely the kit. It is only part of the vast ecosystem of digital products and services we interact with every day. The amount of value any of these things bring to our lives depends on how much they know about us. And the more they know the better they get.

This is the Internet of Me

Of course, there are some obstacles on the road to this utopian future. Security blunders and hacking attacks make us fearful for the safety of our data in others' hands. We are uneasy about the way our information is trawled and traded, then used to track and target us.

So how can we realise the amazing potential of the personal data economy? The answer is surprisingly simple. All it requires is a change in who controls our personal data.

Let's look at health as an example. Here is a sector ripe for innovation but where data is of the most personal and sensitive nature.

Something such as a running app tracks your performance over time and reports your progress relative to your previous runs. It doesn't really tell you much about your fitness beyond this, much less your overall health.

But imagine if your running app was one of many that shared data about your lifestyle. Let's add in your heart rate, sleep pattern, steps walked, food bought, blood pressure, working hours, miles driven. Include your medical records and that data gets seriously deep. The first beneficiary of all this would be you. For the first time you would have a complete picture of your health, fitness and lifestyle.

Through sharing that rich data – or parts of it – between those apps and services (and new ones) you could feed back fresh information that then allows them to further enhance the experience for you.

They could then warn you of potential heath problems, give you lifestyle advice and motivation, and personalise offers for products that could include everything from food to gym memberships to tailored health insurance plans.

Think of any sector and the benefits become obvious – finance, travel, utilities, motoring, retail. Products and services stand to gain so much more relevance and value the more data you put in.

A dysfunctional system

The problem is that right now, businesses have to make do with small nuggets of far inferior data, all different and scattered across countless online services. And the way it is used has led to a war of attrition, with businesses deploying cookies, tracking and targeting algorithms and consumers defending with ad blockers, misinformation or disappearing off the radar altogether.

The resulting marketing methods are crude and annoying, not to mention downright creepy when a business you've never dealt with before seems to know too much about you.

Further frustrating efforts to gain deeper insight into consumers' lives is data protection legislation, the understandable response by governments to public fears over threats to privacy.

Whatever its shortcomings, though, this data is hugely valuable. However, the personal data economy could be so much more. Businesses are only too aware of the massive potential for innovation and growth – and, of course, profit – if they had access to truly rich data. And despite their fears, consumers do want the sort of future it could offer them. It is their sense of powerlessness that is the brake on progress.

A new model

This is where a new model is needed.

The solution is, surely, a shift in ownership and control of personal data back to the consumer. When an individual has all their data together in one place – in a way that would be unimaginable for a third party – the benefits are obvious and immediate. The consumer gets to see the bigger picture with privacy and security. They could then control who is allowed to access and use this complete, rich data, based on what they get in return.

For their part, businesses need to see that this alternative model is better for them too. They would gain access to the kind of data they have only dreamt of. They can then use it to personalise their offer to give consumers exactly what they want. And none of the stuff they don't. The push from business will be matched by pull from consumer.

Platforms such as digi.me that let people aggregate personal data in their own secure place are already there, offering that hallowed 'bigger picture'.

When organisations respect this personal data model and use it to offer greater value and better experiences, people will share yet more data, leading to yet further innovation. It is an opportunity to build ever deeper trust based on mutual benefit. It's what they call a 'win-win' situation.

4 December 2015

⇨ The above information is reprinted with kind permission from digi. me. Please visit http://get.digi.me for further information.

The Internet of Things will be an Internet of obsolete junk

An article from **The Conversation.**

By Toby Miller, Professor of Media & Cultural Studies, Cardiff University

THE CONVERSATION

The US Federal Trade Commission issued a report on the *Internet of Things* this week. It announced:

Six years ago, for the first time, the number of 'things' connected to the Internet surpassed the number of people ... Experts estimate that, as of this year, there will be 25 billion connected devices, and by 2020, 50 billion.

Moments later, UK telecoms regulator Ofcom proclaimed a major initiative to ensure the nation "plays a leading role in developing the Internet of Things.

So the Internet is more than just a topic of work, fun, friends, and family that we routinely mention around the kitchen table; it actually happens there, thanks to such canny innovations as 'smart chopsticks'. These new wonders can detect rancid food and hence protect animal-eating diners from fish-oil infections.

The technocentric promise of this golden age is that electrical appliances will connect to the Internet via subscriber identification modules (SIMs) and radio-frequency identification devices (RFIDs). Technology boosters promise a world where digital wallets will replace cheques and credit cards; personalised electronic adverts will compete with static hoardings; and transport, electricity, power and water systems will provide a continuous real-time update of their performance and user status. Firms will offer us advice and services built on analysis of such data.

The Internet of Things is described as a marvel – the moment when wireless becomes limitless. Building sensors save energy; homes are automated beyond even the vision of post-war suburban idylls; transportation is effortlessly streamlined; smartphone applications direct daily life; manufacturing is tied to merchandising which is tied to consumption; and healthcare occurs at a distance from the bodies being cared for.

The very idea is proclaimed as an expansion of knowledge, convenience, and hence well-being. Cybertarians hail a new age of ethical consumption in which customers know the environmental and labour history and future of the devices and services they purchase and have greater control over their own lives than ever before.

We are at the peak of what the Gartner research firm calls a "hype cycle", when expectations of new technologies rise giddily. This is followed by sober realism and everyday use.

The Design Museum has rapturously announced that we are entering "A New Industrial Revolution". Given the costs as well as the benefits connected to the first one – illness, death, pollution, slavery and war are all there on the downside – one might think the advent of this miraculous new age would provide opportunities to rethink the absurd lightness of being routinely attributed to the Internet.

For the past two decades of cybertarianism have been an era of ignorance. We have neglected the dirty, material origins and processes that characterise communications technologies like tablets, phones and laptops. We have forgotten the real story of Cold War militarism, undersea cables, conflict minerals, slave labour, toxic exposure and illegal recycling. We got such things (the environment, workers and legality) badly wrong the first time, and risk repeating the mistake due to the obfuscatory claims for a post-smokestack Internet age.

Then there are the problems with architecture, security, robustness, interoperability, regulation and privacy across the Internet of things – and doubt even encircles the holy fetish of modernity: economic growth.

In 1987, the year he won the pseudo-Nobel prize for economics, Robert Solow identified what has become known as the 'Solow Paradox'. He came to this insight while reviewing the tide of futurism that accompanied the Cold War and is now reborn via the Internet.

"We are at the peak of what the Gartner research firm calls a 'hype cycle', when expectations of new technologies rise giddily. This is followed by sober realism and everyday use"

Solow doubted the wonders of a service economy, which he thought might produce "a nation of hamburger stands and insurance companies". The memorable phrase he used was: "You can see the computer age everywhere but in the productivity statistics."

Last year, the National Bureau of Economic Research published findings that buttress Solow's Paradox, a decade after it was supposedly dispatched to the dustbin of history courtesy of the Internet. This research suggests that unemployment hastens productivity growth, not information technology. And of course,

the Internet of Things will see labour displaced onto customers, who will become increasingly responsible for work previously undertaken by full-service utilities providers, for example, through properly-employed experts.

"Your light switch, toothbrush, trousers, tights, kettle, bedroom toys – and chopsticks – will be rendered useless thanks to software upgrades, otherwise known as built-in obsolescence"

And what about the instant purchase and upgrade fetishes that will add massive over-consumption to mass capitalism's inexorable crises of overproduction? The Internet of Things will create a mountain of junk. Its electronic detritus will be untold.

Suddenly your light switch, toothbrush, trousers, tights, kettle, bedroom toys – and chopsticks – will be rendered useless thanks to software upgrades, otherwise known as built-in obsolescence.

And that fish-oil prophylactic – do you need it? Why not cease industrial fishing?

28 January 2015

⇨ The above information is reprinted with kind permission from *The Conversation*. Please visit www.theconversation.com for further information.

Internet will isolate 700,000 elderly people by 2030, study warns

Campaign launched by Friends of the Elderly charity warns that the number of older people feeling lonely is set to rise by 40 per cent by 2030.

By Edward Malnick

Hundreds of thousands of pensioners will be all but cut off from government services, shops and local communities within 15 years because of the rise of the Internet, a campaign backed by David Cameron warns.

A study found that a growing shift by banks, utility companies, shops and community groups to carrying out their activities on the web will leave 703,000 over-60s remaining offline at the end of the next decade in situations akin to "living in a home with no windows".

The research showed that the number of older people feeling lonely will rise by 40 per cent by 2030.

The report, published by the Friends of the Elderly charity, concluded that around seven million over-60s would be reporting loneliness in 2030, compared to 5.25 million today.

The charity said the increase would be fuelled by a steep growth in the size of the elderly population, together with a decline in marriage, which will leave more people over 60 living alone.

A separate poll commissioned by the charity found that eight in ten people have irregular or no contact with older people, while more than 50 per cent say they do not know their neighbours well enough to have a conversation with them.

On Thursday, Friends of the Elderly launches a campaign, Be a Friend, based on the research and backed by the Prime Minister, to encourage people across Britain to initiate "everyday interactions" with older neighbours and family members to help combat loneliness. It hopes that the initiative will help to reduce the projected increase in the number of older people feeling lonely.

Its analysis, based on official population figures and the English Longitudinal Study of Ageing, found that 5.25 million people over 60 – or one in three – report feeling lonely at least sometimes. If nothing is done to tackle the problem, the number will rise to 7.03 million by 2030, based on the expected increase in the number of older people as well as the growing number of those living alone.

The study, *The Future of Loneliness*, conducted by the Future Foundation, found that the proportion of people over 65 who use the Internet at home would rise from 51 per cent today to 85-90 per cent by 2030. Friends of the Elderly said it showed that it was vital to take action now to overcome loneliness in order people.

It warned that the digital shift would leave around 703,000 older people at a "serious risk of intensified exclusion" from society if more was not done to get people online.

The warning comes after Francis Maude, the Cabinet Office minister, said in June that in the future most public services would only be available on the Internet "because we think that is a better thing for people's lives".

Steve Allen, chief executive of Friends of the Elderly, said: "To be offline in 2030 will be like living in a home with no windows. We'll miss out on much of the life and conversations of community, on opportunities to buy, sell and take part, and day-to-day shopping and payment of bills will become costlier and more inconvenient.

"As the benefits grow for Internet users, digital exclusion, for non-users, will become increasingly punishing."

The South West has the highest proportion of lonely older people per household, with one on four homes containing someone over 60 who reports feeling lonely. London has the lowest proportion at one in 11.

6 August 2014

⇨ The above information is reprinted with kind permission from *The Telegraph*. Please visit www.telegraph.co.uk for further information.

China has made obedience to the State a game

China has created a social tool which gives people a score for how good a citizen they are.

By Samuel Osborne

With a concept straight out of a cyberpunk dystopia, China has gamified obedience to the State.

China has created a social tool named Sesame Credit which gives people a score for how good a citizen they are.

The system measures how obediently citizens follow the party line, pulling data from social networks and online purchase histories.

As Extra Credits explains on YouTube: "If you post pictures of Tiananmen Square or share a link about the recent stock market collapse, your Sesame Credit goes down.

"Share a link from the state-sponsored news agency about how good the economy is doing and your score goes up."

Similarly, Sesame Credit can analyse data from online purchases.

"If you're making purchases the state deems valuable, like work shoes or local agricultural products, your score goes up.

"If you import anime from Japan though, down the score goes."

Most insidious of all, the app will have real world consequences. According to Extra Credits, high scores will grant users benefits: "Like making it easier to get the paperwork you need to travel or making it easier to get a loan."

> **"If you're making purchases the state deems valuable, like work shoes or local agricultural products, your score goes up... If you import anime from Japan though, down the score goes"**

Although the ratings are currently optional, the social tool will become mandatory by 2020.

There have even been rumours about implementing penalties for low scores: "Like slower Internet speeds, or restricting jobs a low-scoring person is allowed to hold."

The system could also become a powerful tool for social conditioning, as users could lose points for having friends with low obedience scores.

There has already been some evidence of Chinese citizens competing with one another to get high scores, posting their Sesame Credit scores on Weibo, the Chinese equivalent of Twitter, Quartz reports.

Earlier this year, the BBC reported the Chinese Government was building a "social credit" system to rate each citizen's trustworthiness.

A planning document from China's State Council explained the credit will "forge a public opinion environment that trust-keeping is glorious" and warned the "new system will reward those who report acts of breach of trust".

22 December 2015

⇨ The above information is reprinted with kind permission from *The Independent*. Please visit www.independent.co.uk for further information.

WOW - YOUR SOCIAL CREDIT IS HUGE!!

...WANT TO BUY A COMBINE HARVESTER?

How Facebook and Twitter changed missing child searches

Every second counts when a child disappears and social media sites can help speed up investigations.

By Bella Qvist

Every three minutes a child is reported missing in the UK; across the EU that number rises to one child every two minutes. In the US, the FBI recorded almost 467,000 missing children in 2014, which is close to one reported every minute.

In the US, milk cartons, posters, flyers, meetings and traditional news reports formed the main missing child search channels until 1996, when Dallas-Fort Worth broadcasters teamed up with local police to develop a warning system that interrupted regular programming on television and radio broadcasts, and highway signs.

The service, Amber Alert, is used only for the most serious of cases, sending out messages via email, text, traffic signs and digital billboards, as well as through Twitter and Facebook.

International non-profit organisation Action Against Abduction long pressed for a similar system in the UK, but it wasn't until 2012, after the abduction of April Jones, that Child Rescue Alert was activated nationally.

Parents, is it OK to spy on your child's online search history?

In 2015, Child Rescue Alert partnered with Facebook to harness the social network's reach. Now, when a missing child case meets certain criteria of seriousness, law enforcement agencies can issue geo-targeted posts, containing a photo and description, to appear in the newsfeeds of Facebook users in the area where the child is believed to be.

"All over the world, we've seen communities rallying together in times of need, using Facebook to spread the word – and these alerts will make that quicker and help to reach more people than ever before," said Emily Vacher, trust and safety manager at Facebook at the September launch.

"Time is often a crucial element when locating vulnerable missing people who are at risk to themselves or to the public," says Metropolitan Police commander Alison Newcomb. "The use of social media supports our investigations and appeals and has achieved great results, some of which simply could not have happened through traditional communication channels."

Newcomb says the Met operates more than 400 Twitter accounts, but also works closely with other agencies.

"One of the many reasons that the police come to us to help with publicity is that we have this wide network on Twitter and Facebook," says Polly Balsom, communications manager at Missing People.

Gavin Portnoy, head of digital media at the National Center for Missing & Exploited Children, which makes active use of Facebook, Twitter, YouTube, Instagram and Snapchat, has proof of the power of sharing.

In 2015, the charity created a video appeal featuring imagery of a missing girl and the person they suspected had kidnapped her. The video was shared widely and a woman spotted them.

"People feel empowered to make a difference; it's the opportunity to do something," he says.

Another example is the case of Bella Bond, a three-year-old girl whose body was washed up on the shores near Boston, US. Her identity was confirmed following an extensive social media campaign in which a computer-generated composite image was estimated to have reached 47 million people on Facebook.

"It was definitely one of those cases where we can say with great confidence that because it went viral and because as many people interacted with it, it got in front of the eyes of the right person who said 'Oh my goodness, I know that girl'," Portnoy says.

Although social media has provided police and other agencies with extended publicity tools, those same tools can also put children at risk. In Sweden, for example, a man got thousands of people to share his unofficial Facebook appeal for his missing children, but the children were living with their mother who was understood to be under protection with a new identity after leaving the man.

Geoff Newiss, director of research at Action Against Abduction, says that when it comes to searching for children in abduction cases, which can be more complex than missing child cases, social media has been more of a good addition than a game changer.

"There is certainly an increase in cases where the grooming is facilitated by online contact, so in that sense technology provides risks," he says, adding that teachers need more resources to educate children about this, and that the old "stranger danger" advice needs to be updated.

Portnoy, however, says that while he recognises that social media is by no means a perfect tool, its benefits should be acknowledged. "[It] is another really positive tool that's in the arsenal of the public, of law enforcement, of non-profits like us that are trying to help."

27 January 2016

⇨ The above information is reprinted with kind permission from *The Guardian*. Please visit www.theguardian.com for further information.

How digital tech is improving women's health and well-being in India

By Vicki Hearn, Director of Nominet Trust, the UK's largest 'tech for good' funder

Each March, communities across the world celebrate International Women's Day, a campaign highlighting the social, economic, cultural and political achievements of women globally. With the World Economic Forum recently extending the predicted date that gender equality will be achieved by nearly 40 years (from 2096 to 2133), it's particularly poignant that the 2016 campaign theme is #PledgeForParity.

One of the leading barometers for global gender parity is the United Nations Development Programme's Gender Inequality Index, which measures a number of factors such as women's reproductive health, empowerment and labour market participation. Currently lagging in 130th place on this Index, and in the bottom 60 countries, is India. But things are changing.

India is at a pivotal point in its history. As the world's fastest-growing economy, Internet access across India is rapidly increasing and, by 2017, it's expected to become the second largest smartphone market on the planet.

With the dual effect of enhanced access to digital solutions helping to improve women's health and well-being, combined with support for the rise in entrepreneurship, the stage is set for a movement to address the gender imbalance.

At the forefront of this movement is a growing host of remarkable local digital innovators. Over the last three years, Nominet Trust's quest to find new and inspirational social tech projects for our NT100 showcase has shone a light upon three mobile technology initiatives in India. All led by incredible female entrepreneurs, they are not only radically improving the daily lives of women, but also forming part of a more significant movement towards gender parity.

New beginnings for maternal health

The Mobile Alliance for Maternal Action (MAMA) uses mobile phones to deliver vital health information to new and expectant mothers, supporting programmes in India, Bangladesh and Africa. According to MAMA, India accounts for 17 per cent of global maternal mortality, 27 per cent of global newborn mortality and 25 per cent of global child mortality – the largest share of any country. However, the ubiquity of mobile phones has made possible the introduction of a knowledge-sharing service for young, under-served women, often with low literacy levels, with the aim of reducing often preventable deaths.

In 2014, MAMA launched a programme in the Mumbai slums, partnering with ARMANN, an NGO founded by urogynaecologist, social entrepreneur and TEDx speaker, Dr Aparna Hegde. Known as mMitra (mitra literally meaning 'friend' in Hindi), the digital service sends free pregnancy and child health information to pregnant women and new mothers twice each week, in a language and at a time of their choosing. Information is sent via SMS or as a recorded message, and explains the developmental stage of a child throughout pregnancy and the baby's first year of life. Mothers therefore understand the expected developmental milestones and can identify and seek treatment for potential health issues before they escalate. Within the first few months alone, mMitra had 50,000 subscribers. MAMA hopes to take the programme to scale across India.

Hard life, early death

Diseases such as tuberculosis (TB) can have particularly severe consequences for Indian women during their reproductive years. TB is one of the top five causes of death for adult women aged 20–59 and India has the highest number of TB sufferers globally, with 220,000 total deaths in 2014 according to the World Health Organization.

Once again, however, a determined female entrepreneur is helping to combat the issue. Operation ASHA, an NGO based in New Delhi,

was co-founded by inspirational professor and surgeon, Dr Shelly Batra. In partnership with Microsoft Research, she developed an innovative, portable biometric tracking system called eCompliance that has taken TB treatment to the doorsteps of rural communities and slum dwellers across India.

eCompliance aims to improve successful completion of TB patients' full treatment regimen, reducing the default rate that is contributing to the rise of new, drug-resistant, strains of the disease (MDR-TB). Limited resources and infrastructure mean that health professionals struggle to track their patients comprehensively. As a result, India has the highest prevalence of MDR-TB of any country in the world. Operation ASHA uses fingerprint recognition and SMS messaging to ensure patients are adhering to their treatment regimens. At each clinic visit, both the patient and the healthcare worker scan their fingerprints, medication is dispensed and the treatment is recorded in the system's database. If a patient misses a dose, an SMS message alert is sent to the patient and healthcare worker. The

digitisation of the patient records also enables accurate reports to be produced and allows targeted counselling to be provided.

There are now over 130 community centres in India with eCompliance terminals, and over 220,000 visits have been logged. The default rate for patients on the programme has been reported in the *BMJ Open* as an amazingly low 3.2%, compared with 11.5% at other South Delhi TB treatment centres. The model has now been rolled out in Cambodia, Dominican Republic, Kenya and Uganda.

Empowering women by creating safe public spaces

A survey conducted by the Associated Chambers of Commerce and Industry of India found that 92 per cent of working women across many cities felt insecure, especially at night. One project that aims to empower women by encouraging them to tell their harassment stories is Safecity, a mobile and online community founded by Elsa D'Silva, who was herself inspired by the success of other crowd-mapping initiatives.

Shortly after the now infamous gang rape of a medical student on

a Delhi bus, Elsa devised the idea for women to use a phone app to map hotspots of abuse. Talking to *The Guardian*, she says: "That was when everything lined up and I said to myself: safety and security need to be urgently addressed. Until then, not many of us were even talking about it actively or openly enough, including me. It was that rape that really got me thinking more actively ... then I started to remember the various incidents that had taken place in my own life." Her personal silence broken, D'Silva began to talk to friends: "I realised that every one of them had a story to share, but until then we had never really spoken about it."

Safecity also aims to use the data it collects to inform future urban planning, for example highlighting areas which currently have little or no street lighting. Elsa hopes the project will encourage the Indian Government to improve legislation on gender equality by creating a louder voice for women's safety and rights. Already, over 4,000 stories have been collected on Safecity from 50 Indian cities.

Digital technology is the tool helping these inspirational women respond to challenges surrounding gender inequality. You can find out more about these and others like them at socialtech.org.uk, the world's largest database of tech for good projects.

7 March 2016

⇨ The above information is reprinted with kind permission from Nominet Trust. Please visit www.nominettrust.org.uk for further information.

This article was originally featured on the Huffington Post UK website at http://www.huffingtonpost.co.uk/vicki-hearn/tech-women-india_b_9398532.html.

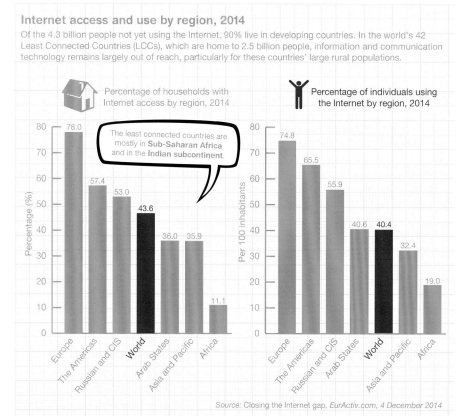

Internet access and use by region, 2014

Of the 4.3 billion people not yet using the Internet, 90% live in developing countries. In the world's 42 Least Connected Countries (LCCs), which are home to 2.5 billion people, information and communication technology remains largely out of reach, particularly for these countries' large rural populations.

Percentage of households with Internet access by region, 2014

The least connected countries are mostly in **Sub-Saharan Africa** and in the **Indian subcontinent**.

Percentage of individuals using the Internet by region, 2014

Source: Closing the Internet gap, *EurActiv.com*, 4 December 2014

Robot law: what happens if intelligent machines commit crimes?

By Jeffrey Wale and David Yuratich, Lecturers in Law

The fear of powerful artificial intelligence and technology is a popular theme, as seen in films such as *Ex Machina*, *Chappie*, and the *Terminator* series.

And we may soon find ourselves addressing fully autonomous technology with the capacity to cause damage. While this may be some form of military wardroid or law enforcement robot, it could equally be something not created to cause harm, but which could nevertheless do so by accident or error. What then? Who is culpable and liable when a robot or artificial intelligence goes haywire? Clearly, our way of approaching this doesn't neatly fit into society's view of guilt and justice.

While some may choose to dismiss this as too far into the future to concern us, remember that a robot has already been arrested for buying drugs. This also ignores how quickly technology can evolve. Look at the lessons from the past – many of us still remember the world before the Internet, social media, mobile technology, GPS – even phones or widely available computers. These once-dramatic innovations developed into everyday technologies which have created difficult legal challenges.

A guilty robot mind?

How quickly we take technology for granted. But we should give some thought to the legal implications. One of the functions of our legal system is to regulate the behaviour of legal persons and to punish and deter offenders. It also provides remedies for those who have suffered or are at risk of suffering harm.

Legal persons – humans, but also companies and other organisations for the purposes of the law – are subject to rights and responsibilities. Those who design, operate, build or sell intelligent machines have legal duties – what about the machines themselves? Our mobile phone, even with Cortana or Siri attached, does not

fit the conventions for a legal person. But what if the autonomous decisions of their more advanced descendents in the future cause harm or damage?

Criminal law has two important concepts. First, that liability arises when harm has been or is likely to be caused by any act or omission. Physical devices such as Google's driverless car, for example, clearly has the potential to harm, kill or damage property. Software also has the potential to cause physical harm, but the risks may extend to less immediate forms of damage such as financial loss.

Second, criminal law often requires culpability in the offender, what is known as the 'guilty mind' or *mens rea* – the principle being that the offence, and subsequent punishment, reflects the offender's state of mind and role in proceedings. This generally means that deliberate actions are punished more severely than careless ones. This poses a problem, in terms of treating autonomous intelligent machines under the law: how do we demonstrate the intentions of a non-human, and how can we do this within existing criminal law principles?

Robocrime?

This isn't a new problem – similar considerations arise in trials of corporate criminality. Some thought needs to go into when, and in what circumstances, we make the designer or manufacturer liable rather than the user. Much of our current law assumes that human operators are involved.

For example, in the context of highways, the regulatory framework assumes that there is a human driver to at least some degree. Once fully autonomous vehicles arrive, that framework will require substantial changes to address the new interactions between human and machine on the road.

As intelligent technology that by-passes direct human control becomes more advanced and more widespread, these questions of risk, fault and punishment will become more pertinent. Film and television may dwell on the most extreme examples, but the legal realities are best not left to fiction.

2 July 2015

⇨ The above information is reprinted with kind permission from Bournemouth University. Please visit www.bournemouth.ac.uk for further information.

⇨ Originally published on *The Conversation*.

Digital life in 2025

Experts predict the Internet will become "like electricity" – less visible, yet more deeply embedded in people's lives for good and ill.

By Jana Anderson and Lee Raine
Pew Research Center

The world is moving rapidly towards ubiquitous connectivity that will further change how and where people associate, gather and share information, and consume media. A canvassing of 2,558 experts and technology builders about where we will stand by the year 2025 finds striking patterns in their predictions. The invited respondents were identified in previous research about the future of the Internet, from those identified by the Pew Research Center's Internet Project, and solicited through major technology-oriented listservs. They registered their answers online between 25 November, 2013 and 13 January, 2014.

In their responses, these experts foresee an ambient information environment where accessing the Internet will be effortless and most people will tap into it so easily it will flow through their lives "like electricity". They predict mobile, wearable and embedded computing will be tied together in the Internet of Things, allowing people and their surroundings to tap into artificial intelligence-enhanced cloud-based information storage and sharing. As Dan Lynch, founder of Interop and former director of computing facilities at SRI International, wrote, "The most useful impact is the ability to connect people. From that, everything flows."

To a notable extent, the experts agree on the technology change that lies ahead, even as they disagree about its ramifications. Most believe there will be:

⇨ A global, immersive, invisible, ambient networked computing environment built through the continued proliferation of smart sensors, cameras, software, databases and massive data centres in a world-spanning information fabric known as the Internet of Things.

⇨ "Augmented reality" enhancements to the real-world input that people perceive through the use of portable/wearable/implantable technologies.

⇨ Disruption of business models established in the 20th century (most notably impacting finance, entertainment, publishers of all sorts and education).

⇨ Tagging, databasing and intelligent analytical mapping of the physical and social realms.

These experts expect existing positive and negative trends to extend and expand in the next decade, revolutionising most human interaction, especially affecting health, education, work, politics, economics and entertainment. Most say they believe the results of that connectivity will be primarily positive. However, when asked to describe the good and bad aspects of the future they foresee, many of the experts can also clearly identify areas of concern, some of them extremely threatening. Heightened concerns over interpersonal ethics, surveillance, terror and crime, may lead societies to question how best to establish security and trust while retaining civil liberties.

Overall, these expert predictions can be grouped into 15 identifiable theses about our digital future – eight of which we characterise as being hopeful, six as concerned, and another as a kind of neutral, sensible piece of advice that the choices that are made now will shape the future. Many involve similar views of the ways technology will change, but differ in their sense of the impact of those technical advances. They are listed below, numbered for the sake of convenience to readers navigating this document, not in a rank ordering.

More-hopeful theses

1) Information sharing over the Internet will be so effortlessly interwoven into daily life that it will become invisible, flowing like electricity, often through machine intermediaries.

David Clark, a senior research scientist at MIT's Computer Science and Artificial Intelligence Laboratory,

noted, "Devices will more and more have their own patterns of communication, their own 'social networks', which they use to share and aggregate information, and undertake automatic control and activation. More and more, humans will be in a world in which decisions are being made by an active set of cooperating devices. The Internet (and computer-mediated communication in general) will become more pervasive but less explicit and visible. It will, to some extent, blend into the background of all we do."

Joe Touch, director at the University of Southern California's Information Sciences Institute, predicted, "The Internet will shift from the place we find cat videos to a background capability that will be a seamless part of how we live our everyday lives. We won't think about 'going online' or 'looking on the Internet' for something – we'll just be online, and just look."

2) The spread of the Internet will enhance global connectivity that fosters more planetary relationships and less ignorance.

Bryan Alexander, senior fellow at the National Institute for Technology in Liberal Education, wrote, "It will be a world more integrated than ever before. We will see more planetary friendships, rivalries, romances, work teams, study groups and collaborations."

Paul Jones, a professor at the University of North Carolina and founder of ibiblio.org, responded, "Television let us see the Global Village, but the Internet let us be actual Villagers."

Tim Bray, an active participant in the Internet Engineering Task Force (IETF) and technology industry veteran, noted, "I expect the miasma of myth and ignorance and conspiracy theory to recede to dark corners of the discourse of civilisation, where nice people don't go. The change in the emotional landscape conferred by people being able to communicate very cheaply irrespective of geography is still only dimly understood."

3) The Internet of Things, artificial intelligence and big data will make people more aware of their world and their own behaviour.

Patrick Tucker, author of *The Naked Future: What Happens In a World That Anticipates Your Every Move?*, wrote, "When the cost of collecting information on virtually every interaction falls to zero, the insights that we gain from our activity, in the context of the activity of others, will fundamentally change the way we relate to one another, to institutions, and with the future itself. We will become far more knowledgeable about the consequences of our actions; we will edit our behaviour more quickly and intelligently."

Judith Donath, a fellow at Harvard University's Berkman Center for Internet and Society, responded, "We'll have a picture of how someone has spent their time, the depth of their commitment to their hobbies, causes, friends and family. This will change how we think about people, how we establish trust, how we negotiate change, failure and success."

4) Augmented reality and wearable devices will be implemented to monitor and give quick feedback on daily life, especially tied to personal health.

Daren C. Brabham, a professor at the Annenberg School for Communication and Journalism, University of Southern California, predicted, "We will grow accustomed to seeing the world through multiple data layers. This will change a lot of social practices, such as dating, job interviewing and professional networking and gaming, as well as policing and espionage."

Aron Roberts, software developer at the University of California-Berkeley, said, "We may well see wearable devices and/or home and workplace sensors that can help us make ongoing lifestyle changes and provide early detection for disease risks, not just disease. We may literally be able to adjust both medications and lifestyle changes on a day-by-day basis or even an hour-by-hour basis, thus enormously

magnifying the effectiveness of an ever more understaffed medical delivery system."

5) Political awareness and action will be facilitated and more peaceful change and public uprisings like the Arab Spring will emerge.

Rui Correia, director of Netday Namibia, a non-profit supporting innovations in information technology for education and development, wrote, "With mobile technologies and information-sharing apps becoming ubiquitous, we can expect some significant improvement in the awareness of otherwise illiterate and ill-informed rural populations to opportunities missed out by manipulative and corrupt governments. Like the Arab Spring, we can expect more and more uprisings to take place as people become more informed and able to communicate their concerns."

Nicole Ellison, an associate professor in the School of Information at the University of Michigan, predicted, "As more of the global population comes online, there will be increased awareness of the massive disparities in access to healthcare, clear water, education, food, and human rights."

6) The spread of the 'Ubernet' will diminish the meaning of borders, and new 'nations' of those with shared interests may emerge and exist beyond the capacity of current nation-states to control.

David Hughes, an Internet pioneer, who from 1972 worked in individual to/from digital telecommunications, responded, "All 7-plus billion humans on this planet will sooner or later be 'connected' to each other and fixed destinations, via the Uber(not Inter)net. That can lead to the diminished power over people's lives within nation-states. When every person on this planet can reach, and communicate two-way, with every other person on this planet, the power of nation-states to control every human inside its geographic boundaries may start to diminish."

JP Rangaswami, chief scientist for Salesforce.com, observed, "The problems that humanity now faces are problems that can't be contained by political borders or economic systems. Traditional structures of government and governance are therefore ill-equipped to create the sensors, the flows, the ability to recognise patterns, the ability to identify root causes, the ability to act on the insights gained, the ability to do any or all of this at speed, while working collaboratively across borders and time zones and sociopolitical systems and cultures. From climate change to disease control, from water conservation to nutrition, from the resolution of immune-system-weakness conditions to solving the growing obesity problem, the answer lies in what the Internet will be in decades to come. By 2025, we will have a good idea of its foundations."

7) The Internet will become 'the Internets' as access, systems and principles are renegotiated.

David Brin, author and futurist, responded, "There will be many Internets. Mesh networks will self-form and we'll deputise sub-selves to dwell in many places."

Sean Mead, senior director of strategy and analytics for Interbrand, predicted, "The Internet will generate several new related networks. Some will require verified identification to access, while others will promise increased privacy."

Ian Peter, pioneer Internet activist and Internet rights advocate, wrote, "The Internet will fragment. Global connectivity will continue to exist, but through a series of separate channels controlled by a series of separate protocols. Our use of separate channels for separate applications will be necessitated by security problems, cyber policy of nations and corporations, and our continued attempts to find better ways to do things."

8) An Internet-enabled revolution in education will spread more opportunities, with less money spent on real estate and teachers.

A generally hopeful summary comes from Doc Searls, journalist and director of ProjectVRM at Harvard's Berkman Center for Internet and Society, who observed, "Of course, there will be bad acting by some,

taking advantage of organisational vulnerabilities and gaming systems in other ways. Organisations in the meantime will continue rationalising negative externalities, such as we see today with pollution of the Internet's pathways by boundless wasted advertising messages, and bots working to game the same business. But … civilisation deals with bad acting through development of manners, norms, laws and regulations. Expect all of those to emerge and evolve over the coming years. But don't expect the Internet to go away … Will the Internet make it possible for our entire civilization to collapse together, in one big awful heap? Possibly. But the Internet has already made it possible for us to use one of our unique graces – the ability to share knowledge – for good, and to a degree never before possible."

Less-hopeful theses

9) Dangerous divides between haves and have-nots may expand, resulting in resentment and possible violence.

Oscar Gandy, an emeritus professor at the Annenberg School, University of Pennsylvania, explained, "We have to think seriously about the kinds of conflicts that will arise in response to the growing inequality enabled and amplified by means of networked transactions that benefit smaller and smaller segments of the global population. Social media will facilitate and amplify the feelings of loss and abuse. They will also facilitate the sharing of examples and instructions about how to challenge, resist and/or punish what will increasingly come to be seen as unjust."

10) Abuses and abusers will 'evolve and scale'. Human nature isn't changing; there's laziness, bullying, stalking, stupidity, pornography, dirty tricks, crime and those who practise them have new capacity to make life miserable for others.

Llewellyn Kriel, CEO and editor in chief of TopEditor International Media Services, predicted, "Everything – every thing – will be available online with price tags attached. Cyber-terrorism will become commonplace. Privacy and confidentiality of any and

all personal will become a thing of the past. Online 'diseases' – mental, physical, social, addictions (psycho-cyber drugs) – will affect families and communities and spread willy-nilly across borders. The digital divide will grow and worsen beyond the control of nations or global organisations such as the UN. This will increasingly polarize the planet between haves and have-nots. Global companies will exploit this polarization. Digital criminal networks will become realities of the new frontiers. Terrorism, both by organizations and individuals, will be daily realities. The world will become less and less safe, and only personal skills and insights will protect individuals."

An antispam and security architect predicted, "There will be an erosion of privacy and the use of dirty-tricks social media will emerge more and more in election campaigns. Abusers evolve and scale far more than regular Internet users."

A retired management consultant to a large international corporation wrote, "There will be greater group-think, group-speak and mob mentality … More uninformed individuals will influence others to the detriment of standard of living and effective government."

11) Pressured by these changes, governments and corporations will try to assert power – and at times succeed – as they invoke security and cultural norms.

Paul Babbitt, an associate professor at Southern Arkansas University, predicted, "Governments will become much more effective in using the Internet as an instrument of political and social control. That is, filters will be increasingly valuable and important, and effective and useful filters will be able to charge for their services. People will be more than happy to trade the free-wheeling aspect common to many Internet sites for more structured and regulated environments."

Anoop Ghanwani, a distinguished engineer at Dell, said, "Regulation will always stand in the way of anything significant happening."

12) People will continue – sometimes grudgingly – to make tradeoffs favouring convenience and perceived immediate gains over privacy; and privacy will be something only the upscale will enjoy.

An anonymous respondent wrote, "Yes, the information we want will increasingly find its way to us, as networks learn to accurately predict our interests and weaknesses. But that will also tempt us to stop seeking out knowledge, narrowing our horizons, even as we delve evermore deep. The privacy premium may also be a factor: only the relatively well-off (and well-educated) will know how to preserve their privacy in 2025."

13) Humans and their current organisations may not respond quickly enough to challenges presented by complex networks.

Randy Kluver, an associate professor of communication at Texas A&M University, responded, "The most neglected aspect of the impact is in the geopolitics of the Internet. There are very few experts focused on this, and yet the rise of digital media promises significant disruption to relations between and among states. Some of the really important dimensions include the development of transnational political actors/ movements, the rise of the virtual state, the impact of digital diplomacy efforts, the role of information in undermining state privilege (think Wikileaks), and … the development of cyber-conflict (in both symmetric and asymmetric forms)."

A librarian shared a quote from Albert Einstein: "It has become appallingly clear that our technology has surpassed our humanity."

14) Most people are not yet noticing the profound changes today's communications networks are already bringing about; these networks will be even more disruptive in the future.

Nishant Shah, visiting professor at the Centre for Digital Cultures at Leuphana University, Germany, observed, "It is going to systemically change our understandings of being human,

being social and being political. It is not merely a tool of enforcing existing systems; it is a structural change in the systems that we are used to. And this means that we are truly going through a paradigm shift – which is celebratory for what it brings, but it also produces great precariousness because existing structures lose meaning and valence, and hence, a new world order needs to be produced in order to accommodate for these new modes of being and operation. The greatest impact of the Internet is what we are already witnessing, but it is going to accelerate."

A summary of the less-hopeful theses comes from Bob Briscoe, chief researcher in networking and infrastructure for British Telecom, who predicted, "The greatest impacts of the Internet will continue to be the side-effects that tower so high that we do not notice they are continuing to grow far above us: 1) More people will lose their grounding in the realities of life and work, instead considering those aspects of the world amenable to expression as information as if they were the whole world. 2) The scale of the interactions possible over the Internet will tempt more and more people into more interactions than they are capable of sustaining, which on average will continue to lead each interaction to be more superficial. 3) Given there is strong evidence that people are much more willing to commit petty crimes against people and organizations when they have no face-to-face interaction, the increasing proportion of human interactions mediated by the Internet will continue the trend toward less respect and less integrity in our relations."

15) Foresight and accurate predictions can make a difference; "The best way to predict the future is to invent it."

Robert Cannon, Internet law and policy expert, wrote, "The Internet, automation and robotics will disrupt the economy as we know it. How will we provide for the humans who can no longer earn money through labour? The opportunities are simply tremendous. Information, the ability to understand that information, and the ability to act on that information will be available ubiquitously … or we

could become a 'brave new world' where the Government (or corporate power) knows everything about everyone everywhere and every move can be foreseen, and society is taken over by the elite with control of the technology … The good news is that the technology that promises to turn our world on its head is also the technology with which we can build our new world. It offers an unbridled ability to collaborate, share and interact. 'The best way to predict the future is to invent it.' It is a very good time to start inventing the future."

Sonigitu Asibong Ekpe, a consultant with the AgeCare Foundation, a non-profit organisation, observed, "The most significant impact of the Internet is getting us to imagine different paths that the future may take. These paths help us to be better prepared for long-term contingencies; by identifying key indicators, and amplifying signals of change, they help us ensure that our decisions along the way are flexible enough to accommodate change… That billions more people are poised to come online in the emerging economies seems certain. Yet much remains uncertain: from who will have access, how, when, and at what price to the Internet's role as an engine for innovation and the creation of commercial, social and human value. As users, industry players and policymakers, the interplay of decisions that we make today and in the near future will determine the evolution of the Internet and the shape it takes by 2025, in both intended and unintended ways. Regardless of how the future unfolds, the Internet will evolve in ways we can only begin to imagine. By allowing ourselves to explore and rehearse divergent and plausible futures for the Internet, not only do we prepare for any future, we can also help shape it for the better."

11 March 2014

"Digital Life in 2025" Pew Research Center, Washington, DC (April, 2014) http://pewinternet.org/2014/03/11/ digital-life-in-2025/

Key facts

⇨ An Institute for Public Policy Research (IPPR) survey found that 80% of young people said it was too easy to access pornography online, and 72% feel that it is leading to unrealistic views about sex – particularly among boys. (page 2)

⇨ A recent report found that 46% of 18-year-olds felt that sending naked pictures to each other – a practice more commonly known as 'sexting' – was "part of everyday life for teenagers nowadays". (page 2)

⇨ Agencies such as ChildLine are suggesting that calls to them about cyberbullying (up 87%) and sexting/ pornography (up 145%) are increasing at alarming rates. (page 2)

⇨ In August 2015 a billion people used Facebook on a single day, a seventh of the world's population. Facebook is seen as the third most significant consumer invention, chosen by 23%. (page 4)

⇨ In 2014 YouGov found that 84% of 18–24s had used Wikipedia for professional or academic research, compared to only 49% of 40–59 year olds. (page 4)

⇨ 82% of 11-18-year-old respondents to an online survey said that they used a smartphone on a weekly basis, compared to 9% who said they use a normal mobile on a weekly basis. (page 5)

⇨ 95% of 11–18 year old respondents to an online survey said they have downloaded apps. (page 5)

⇨ 83% of respondents to an online survey said their parent pays their phone bill, while 17% said they pay for their bill themselves. There are no statistically significant gender differences. (page 5)

⇨ Children aged 12–15 are turning away from talking on the telephone. Just 3% of their communications time is spent making voice calls, while the vast majority (94%) is text based – such as instant messaging and social networking. (page 6)

⇨ 20% of UK adults' communications time is spent on the phone on average. (page 6)

⇨ Over four in ten households (44%) now have a tablet. (page 6)

⇨ Young adults are glued to their smartphones for 3 hours 36 minutes each day, nearly three times the 1 hour 22 minute average across all adults. (page 6)

⇨ While technology is seen by many as a distraction in our daily lives, a quarter (24%) of workers think technology is improving their work-life balance. Just under half (49%) say it is not making much difference either way and 16% think technology is making their work-life balance worse. (page 7)

⇨ A survey of 13- to 18-year-olds found 24% reported they were targeted on the Internet because of their gender, sexual orientation, race, religion, disability or transgender identity. (page 8)

⇨ More than four in five (82%) youngsters have seen or heard "online hate" in the previous 12 months, with 41% suggesting it had become more rife. (page 8)

⇨ Researchers found that: 74% of teens had unfriended and 58% had blocked other users to avoid sharing information with them; 60% of teens kept their profile private; 58% said they shared inside jokes or cloaked their messages in some way; 57% decided not to post something online because it may have had negative consequences for them in the future; and 26% reported false information to help protect their privacy. (page 15)

⇨ YouGov research from 2014 shows that 81% of UK 13–18-year-olds own their own smartphone, with 34% also owning a tablet. Primary-aged children are equally tech savvy, with statistics from the same year recording that 25% of children own their own tablet before the age of eight and 70% are confident in using mobile devices by the time they go to school. (page 17)

⇨ 37 per cent of parents asked said that their child spent between one and two hours a day playing with tech gadgets, and 28 per cent said between two and three hours. Moreover, 38 percent of two- to five-year-olds own an Android tablet, and 32 per cent own an iPad; almost a third (32 per cent) of these kids also have a mobile phone. (page 19)

⇨ Children aged 12–15 are spending more time online (rising from 14.9 hours a week to 17.1 hours) and spend as much time in a week using the Internet as they do watching television. (page 20)

⇨ Up to 43 per cent of kids are also more likely to mostly use the Internet in their bedrooms. (page 21)

⇨ 5.25 million people over 60 – or one in three – report feeling lonely at least sometimes. If nothing is done to tackle the problem, the number will rise to 7.03 million by 2030, based on the expected increase in the number of older people as well as the growing number of those living alone. (page 30)

Blue light

Experts believe that long-term exposure to blue light can damage the eye. It has also been linked to poor sleep as it disrupts your body's natural rhythm.

Bring your own device (BYOD)

A scheme employed by schools in which they encourage pupils to bring their own devices into the classroom, to be used as part of lessons. For example tablets and smartphones.

Digital footprint

The 'trail' a person leaves behind when they interact with the digital environment. This evidence left behind gives clues as to the person's existence, presence and identify. It also refers to what other people may say about you online, not just yourself: sometimes also referred to as your online presence.

Digital native

A person who has grown up surrounded by digital technology, such as mobile phones, computers and the Internet (the current 12- to 18-year-old generation).

Facebook

Facebook is a social media platform that allows people to connect with one another, set up profiles, share photos and post updates about what they are doing.

In-app purchasing

This refers to purchases made 'within' an app. For example, if you download a free app and are then asked to buy 'upgrades' that allow you more lives or access to different parts of the game. Often, children make accidental purchases through their parents' accounts when devices remember passwords and account information.

Internet

A worldwide system of interlinked computers, all communicating with each other via phone lines, satellite links, wireless networks and cable systems.

Screen time

A term used to refer to the amount of time someone (usually young children) spend in front of a screen. For example, a tablet, smartphone or computer.

Sexting

The exchange of sexually explicit photographs or messages via mobile phone.

Social media

Websites or apps that allow people to create and share social content with one another.

Social networking sites

A place online where people, usually with similar interests, hobbies or backgrounds, can build social networks and social relations together. Examples include websites such as Facebook, Twitter and Pinterest.

Superfast broadband

Superfast broadband is defined as providing download speeds of over 24 Mbps. Currently, the Government aims to have superfast broadband available in 95% of UK premises by the end of 2017 but many rural areas are still struggling with very low download speeds.

Technology addiction

A compulsive need to use technology like smartphones, smartwatches, computers, video games, etc.

The Internet of Things

This term refers to the network of objects that now connect via the Internet. For example, cars, watches, fridges, etc.

Trolling

Troll is Internet slang for someone who intentionally posts something online to provoke a reaction. The idea behind the trolling phenomenon is that it is about humour, mischief and, some argue, freedom of speech; it can be anything from a cheeky remark to a violent threat. However, sometimes these Internet pranks can be taken too far, such as a person who defaces Internet tributes site, causing the victim's family further grief.

Twitter

A social networking site that allows people to post 'tweets' (updates) of no more than 140 characters.

Assignments

Brainstorming

⇨ In small groups, discuss what you know about the Internet of Things.

  • What does the term 'Internet of Things' refer to?

  • What kind of things are included in this definition?

Research

⇨ Talk to a relative who is in their 50s, or older. Find out how technology has changed since they were your age. Ask about their first experiences of using the Internet. Make some notes and create an engaging presentation to share with your class.

⇨ Conduct a survey among your year group to find out what people consider to be the most important technological innovation of the last ten years. Is it smartphones? E-readers? Netflix? Create a bar chart to display your findings.

⇨ Research the harmful effects of blue light and write a bullet point list of your findings.

⇨ Conduct a survey amongst your friends and family to find out how many people of different age groups have experienced being trolled online.

⇨ Read the article *How Facebook and Twitter changed missing child searches* on page 32 and do some research to find out about other ways social media has positively impacted upon society.

Design

⇨ Create a 'how-to' guide for an older person who has just bought a smartphone. Introduce them to some apps you think they might find useful, and explain how they work.

⇨ Choose one of the articles from this book and create an illustration that highlights the key themes of the piece.

⇨ Design a guide for parents that explains the dangers of in-app purchasing, and how to avoid receiving unwanted costly bills.

⇨ Create a campaign to raise awareness of the effects of being trolled and abused online. Your campaign could take the form of posters, YouTube videos, website banners or Facebook adverts. Write 500 words about how your campaign will work and include illustrations to demonstrate your concept.

Oral

⇨ "Children today would be better off without the Internet." Divide your class in half and debate this statement, with half arguing in favour and half arguing against.

⇨ In pairs, discuss what you think the age of consent for social media platforms like Facebook and Twitter should be. Feedback to your class.

⇨ What impact has the Internet had on people's privacy? Discuss in pairs.

⇨ Do you believe it is OK for parents to spy on their children's online search history? Discuss this question in pairs and create a list of reasons why it is OK and why it is not OK. Share with your class.

⇨ Create a PowerPoint presentation that will persuade your headteacher of the benefits of allowing pupils to bring their own devices to school.

⇨ In small groups, think about some of the difficulties older people might experience in a more technology-based future. List some things they might struggle with. For example, online banking or apps that allow you to pay your car parking fee.

Reading/writing

⇨ Imagine that you live in a village where you cannot access super fast broadband. Write a letter to your local MP explaining why it is important for the residents of your village to have their broadband upgraded.

⇨ Try locking your smartphone in a drawer for at least three hours one evening this week. Make some notes about how you feel during this time. Are you anxious? Is it difficult to leave the phone there and resist checking it? What are you thinking about? Write a summary of your experience and share with your class.

⇨ Write an article for your school newspaper exploring the impact of technology on young people's quality of sleep.

⇨ Imagine you are an Agony Aunt/Uncle and that someone has written to you with fears that their son/daughter is addicted to using their smartphone. Write a helpful reply.

⇨ Choose a film or television series that explores issues of artificial intelligence and write a review of its key themes.

⇨ Read *China has made obedience to the State a game* on page 31 and write a short-story exploring what it might be like to live in a futuristic British society where a toll like Sesame Credit exists.

Acknowledgements

The publisher is grateful for permission to reproduce the material in this book. While every care has been taken to trace and acknowledge copyright, the publisher tenders its apology for any accidental infringement or where copyright has proved untraceable. The publisher would be pleased to come to a suitable arrangement in any such case with the rightful owner.

Images

All images courtesy of iStock, except page 6 © Ryan McGuire, page 9 © Rock Cohen, page 25 © Life of Pix and page 35 © Siyan Ren.

Icons on pages 2, 7, 19 and 34 made by Freepik from www. flaticon.com

Icons on page 21, clockwise from the phone icon, made by: Zurb, Freepik, Yannick, Freepik, Freepik, Daniel Bruce, Freepik, Freepik, Freepik, Elegant Themes, Freepik, Freepik, Freepik, SimpleIcon, Google, Catalin Fertu Illustrations, from www.flaticon.com.

Illustrations

Don Hatcher: pages 1 & 29. Simon Kneebone: pages 18 & 31. Angelo Madrid: pages 20 & 33.

Additional acknowledgements

Editorial on behalf of Independence Educational Publishers by Cara Acred.

With thanks to the Independence team: Mary Chapman, Sandra Dennis, Christina Hughes, Jackie Staines and Jan Sunderland.

Cara Acred

Cambridge

May 2016